The bit before the actual beginning…

An Englishman, a Scotsman and an Irishman walked into a bar. The barman looked them up and down and said, *'Is this some sort of joke?'*

All gags started like that in the 1970s and 80s. They were hilarious, until we found out that they were actually lazy, stereotypical, racial slurs. Who knew? Alternative comedy brushed these tired *olde worlde* jokes aside, so we had to come up with something different.

tea cosy, doesn't try it on.

Billy Connolly

Which is fine by us because nobody tells jokes any more. It's all about stories, and our story didn't start like that. There was no Irishman. And no bar. There was an Englishman and a Scotsman, but they met in a café at St Andrews. They had a cup of tea, a bit of a natter and left it at that.

That doesn't work as a gag (not even an alternative one) and is not even vaguely interesting.

But what follows is. Because, you see, the Englishman and Scotsman kept in touch and when the time was right, they joined forces to write a book. This book, as it happens.

So what exactly is 'this book'?

This book, dear reader, is the best self-help book ever written. By Gav and Andy, that is. Whether it's actually the best ever, I guess the Amazon reviews will be the judge of that. Hand on heart, our aim at the outset was to write the best damned book the self-help shelves have ever seen.

The Scotsman was excited. You see, he's never written a book before, so had no idea what pain and suffering was down the line. The gnarled old Englishman's an old hand. He knew, so his excitement was tinged with scepticism. *'The best book ever'* was a nice idea (it was the Scotsman's idea), but really? The Englishman smiled politely, like we do.

Anyhow, the Englishman and Scotsman came up with a plan and went their separate ways. Gav to Edinburgh, Andy to Derby, and they started penning stuff. Well typing it, but you know what I mean

The Englishman was struggling a bit. He was beginning to wonder how many times he could get away with saying *exactly* the same thing that he'd said in his previous five books, when *'ping'*, an email arrived. It was the Scotsman. *'Will be sending you some ideas later today.'*

That was it.

Ten minutes later; *ping*, another email from Edinburgh, entitled 'A wee bit of magic', and this time there was an attachment.

I sighed. 'A wee bit of magic'? *Wee?* The Scotsman is writing it in chuffing Scottish!

I was about to open the attachment when there were two more *pings*; 'Silly Stress' and 'Mary Poppins' had arrived, each with an attachment.

The Scotsman was flying.

I opened 'A wee bit of magic' and had a quick look. In a previous life Gav had been a teacher, plus I've heard him deliver a keynote and I'd read his back catalogue of blogs, so I knew he was okay with words. But he's unpublished.

'A wee bit of magic' blew me away. In two short pages, I laughed and cried.

Beginner's luck?

I clicked on 'Silly Stress'. *Same!* 'Mary Poppins' raised the already sky-high self-help bar to Dick Fosbury levels. It was flopping amazing; a proper sucker punch of writing that softened me up with some fun stuff before delivering a killer blow that took the wind out of me. It was the kind of writing that I had always wanted to do.

The best self-help book the world had ever seen? What if the Scotsman was being serious?

While the Englishman was reading, six more emails had winged their way down the A1/M18/M1 information superhighway, each as good as the last.

And so here we are. It's clear that the Scotsman probably didn't need the Englishman at all. Or maybe he did? Because the seemingly random bunch of stories needed a narrative. There are times when the reader needs a breather, and that's where I come in with a bit of science or a new angle, or (as is very often the case but will go totally unnoticed) some proper punctuation. Apostrophes? *Helloooo!* I wonder how the Scotsman ever qualified as a teacher. So, for the purists, I promise good grammar and no emojis. Thinking aloud, is it a generational thing – putting three exclamation marks to make a really big point?!?!?!

A new word for you

Mephobia: the fear of being so awesome that the human race can't handle it and everybody dies.

Anyhow, there's a lesson for you already in the comparison thing that I've been doing. Gav talks about changing your focus away from being the best *in* the world towards being the best *for* the world. It's a subtle play on words that has very unsubtle connotations. It dovetails rather snugly with Simon Sinek's notion that finite players play to beat the people around them whereas *infinite* players play to be better than themselves. Applying it to life means it's not about Twitter followers, FB likes, book sales, salary earned or how funny you are. It's not about producing better work than your colleagues, or outdoing anyone. One-upmanship gets you disliked.

Matching up to the Scotsman's levels of hilarity is beyond me, so I swapped 'finite' for 'infinite' thinking. Whether I can write books that are as amazing as the ones my heroes write becomes a moot point. I've changed my focus. The greatest personal development writers of all time are not my competition. The Scotsman is not my competition.

I am my competition. Not just in writing, but in everything.

And you are yours.

In which case, joy doesn't come from comparison, but from advancement. For me, it's about producing better work than I did last time. I'm very very proud of my previous books. That means I have to up my game to be very very *very* proud of this one.

Best of all, it's actually quite a relief to twig that I don't have to match up against the best in the world. I only have to match up to being a little bit better than me from last time. It helps enormously to have the flying Scotsman on board because he will help me be better.

And if I can help him too, we're cool.

So there you go, your first lesson and we haven't even got to Chapter 1 yet. *Progression rather than comparison.*

And so to the actual book itself…

SHINE

SHINE

Rediscovering your energy, happiness & purpose

Andy Cope & Gavin Oattes

WILEY

This edition first published 2018

© 2018 Andy Cope and Gavin Oattes

Registered office

John Wiley & Sons Ltd, The Atrium, Southern Gate, Chichester, West Sussex, PO19 8SQ, United Kingdom

For details of our global editorial offices, for customer services and for information about how to apply for permission to reuse the copyright material in this book please see our website at www.wiley.com.

All rights reserved. No part of this publication may be reproduced, stored in a retrieval system, or transmitted, in any form or by any means, electronic, mechanical, photocopying, recording or otherwise, except as permitted by the UK Copyright, Designs and Patents Act 1988, without the prior permission of the publisher.

Wiley publishes in a variety of print and electronic formats and by print-on-demand. Some material included with standard print versions of this book may not be included in e-books or in print-on-demand. If this book refers to media such as a CD or DVD that is not included in the version you purchased, you may download this material at http://booksupport.wiley.com. For more information about Wiley products, visit www.wiley.com.

Designations used by companies to distinguish their products are often claimed as trademarks. All brand names and product names used in this book are trade names, service marks, trademarks or registered trademarks of their respective owners. The publisher is not associated with any product or vendor mentioned in this book.

Limit of Liability/Disclaimer of Warranty: While the publisher and author have used their best efforts in preparing this book, they make no representations or warranties with respect to the accuracy or completeness of the contents of this book and specifically disclaim any implied warranties of merchantability or fitness for a particular purpose. It is sold on the understanding that the publisher is not engaged in rendering professional services and neither the publisher nor the author shall be liable for damages arising herefrom. If professional advice or other expert assistance is required, the services of a competent professional should be sought.

Library of Congress Cataloging-in-Publication Data is available

A catalogue record for this book is available from the British Library.

ISBN 978-0-857-08765-2 (pbk) ISBN 978-0-857-08761-4 (ebk)
ISBN 978-0-857-08764-5 (ebk)

10 9 8 7 6 5 4 3 2 1

Cover Design and Illustrations: Amy Bradley
Cover Image: © TANAKORN6335/Shutterstock

Set in 10/14 Frutiger LT Std by Aptara

Printed in Great Britain by TJ International Ltd, Padstow, Cornwall, UK

*Thank you to my wife Ali, who always tells me I can
just when I need to believe it.*

*This book is for the over thinkers, the worriers and anyone else in the
world who turned red while reading aloud in class.*

– Gavin Oattes

CONTENTS

Chapter 1
THIIIIIS MUCH EXCITED

Page 1

Chapter 2
A RACE TO THE BOTTOM?

time to get your SHINE on!

Page 25

Chapter 3
A SPOONFUL OF SUGAR

Mary Poppins vs Mr Banks

Page 51

Chapter 4
THAT WEE PIECE OF MAGIC

you're it

Page 75

Chapter 5
TRIPLETS WILL ALMOST
CERTAINLY CHANGE YOUR LIFE

Coulda,
woulda,
shoulda

Page 95

Chapter 6
SHINING ON THE
INSIDE

At your Service...

Page 117

Chapter 7
THE SHINE TOP 10

Page 137

Chapter 8
CARRY ON THINKING

fishy business awaits you →

Page 163

Chapter 9
UNRAVELLING
STRING THEORY

Spot the similarity...

Page 183

Chapter 10
A NEW BEGINNING

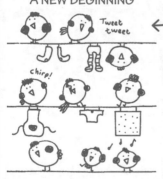

Tweet tweet

chirp!

Page 203

Chapter 1
THIIIIIS MUCH EXCITED

What's it to be? Same old shit, or crazy new shit?

Welcome to the crazy new variety, in which Chapter 1 is introduced by a 5-year-old and we grapple with the concept of 'normal' and 'shine o'clock'.

Then it's adults only. We go all 50 Shades, with an explanation about why there's less sex in the city. We check out Andy's unremarkable breasts and his super-keen sense of smell before sloshing around in Thailand.

Then there's this book, that book, bad books and a very good book (with a towel) which explains what SHINE is all about. Kind of.

And if giving you less to think about isn't enough, we throw in what we're calling a 'Bilbo Bagginsism' before challenging you with the ultimate question: 'are you a wild salmon or stickleback kind of person?'

After toasting your good self we turn to births, marriages and deaths and invite you to hang around at your own funeral. Even in ghostly form you have choices – you could be death-eatery (dark and foreboding), polter geisty (knocking on doors and shifting the vases) or Casper-like (floaty and friendly). We favour the latter. In a bizarre chapter ending, we offer up the ultimate challenge – to light up your own funeral.

Shine baby, shine!

Shine o'clock

Gav will never forget his son's first day at school, which was, bizarrely, a Friday. It was a two-hour taster visit and then he'd start his first full day the following week. Fair dos.

> 'You'll turn out ordinary if you're not careful.'
> *Ann Brashares*

I woke up on the *Monday* of that week to discover Kian stood beside me at 6am dressed in full school uniform. I reminded him that his first day was, in fact, Friday. 'I know,' he replied firmly, 'I'm practising.'

He also practised Tuesday, Wednesday and Thursday, standing at the foot of my bed, ship-shape and inspection ready at 6am. He forgot on the actual Friday because he was exhausted by his unbroken run of early mornings, but that's not the point.

I woke him on Friday and he leaped out of bed, threw his uniform on and came sprinting into our room. Ali and I smiled weary, early-morning-parenting smiles. I told Kian that I'd never seen him this excited before in his entire life.

He agreed wholeheartedly: 'That's because I've never been this excited in my entire life.' There was a brief pause before he delivered the best bit: 'And I've been alive for five years!' His eyes grew wider and he rose to his tiptoes in glee. 'In fact, Dad, I'll show you how excited I am. I am *THIIIIIS MUCH* EXCITED!'

Please picture a five-year-old with his arms stretched so wide his hands are almost clasped behind his back, shoulder blades touching. If you're struggling, imagine an angler who'd caught a very big fish but was also prone to gross exaggeration, and you're in the right ball park.

You can probably remember being five. Pretty much everything's exciting at that age, so to be beyond 'normal' excitement and to have ventured into '*THIIIIIS much* excited' – we're in 'unmitigated joy' territory.

That morning, my wife and I had a wonderful discussion about how, in that moment, there were thousands of young kids all waking up feeling the same – buzzing, pumped and ready to go. Raring to throw themselves into the next step of life's adventure.

We continued to talk about how amazing it is that some people remain like that throughout life. Every single springy step of the journey – the infectious energy, the buzz, the SHINE. And then we had a really weird discussion about how some people never feel like that again. Their wee piece of magic dwindles, it fizzles and vanishes. It's like your rice krispies that you poured milk on and forgot. An hour later, their snap, crackle and pop is just a mushy mess.

Could it be that some people peak at five?

There is, of course, a downside to taking the next step in your adventure. Fear. Worry. Stress. Anxiety. You are excited and yet it's tinged with what might go wrong. It might not work. You know the oft-trotted mantra of 'failure is not an option' is bullshit. Failure is an actual thing. You know because you've experienced it.

But when you're four or five – even though you're a little scared – you're *THIIIIIS much* excited.

BRING. IT. ON!

So, what about you? Did you wake up this morning feeling *THIIIIIS much* excited? Or are you the angler that caught the stickleback of joy?

How often do you wake up on a Monday morning pumped, buzzing and raring to go? Are you waking up every single day energized, happy, driven and frothing with passion? We're not talking about some days or most days, we mean EVERY SINGLE DAY!

If your answer is 'No' then there's a word for people like you: *normal*.

It's absolutely normal. It's normal *not* to wake up every day genuinely pumped full of energy, buzzing, raring to go.

In work it's normal too. It's normal for an organization NOT to have all its people waking up every morning fit to burst with excitement at the prospect of going to work and banging out world-class customer service. If you skip into work 'frothing with passion', someone's going to be making you a doctor's appointment.

Think about this for a moment.

It's normal. You're normal.

It is now the norm NOT to have people waking up energized, buzzing and raring to go to work. To go do the things they have chosen to do, every single day.

I'm going to say it once more.

It's normal. And it doesn't sit well with me. So here are a couple of rhetoricals to get your juices flowing.

Firstly, *what good is having a belly if there's no fire in it?*

And secondly, *do you want 'normal'?*

I'm willing to put money on it that every single person reading this book absolutely categorically does NOT want normal.

I'm willing to wager that you are, in fact, looking for, working for, hoping for, striving for, dreaming about something absolutely extraordinary. Something exciting, engaging, purposeful, colourful – even a little bit scary. Something that makes a difference.

Something that makes you feel *THIIIIIS much* excited.

Can you imagine what would happen if you woke up every single day with the same fire in your belly for the day ahead that you had when you were five?

> 'Great minds think alike, but are usually a bit mad.'
>
> Hannibal, 'A-Team'

It would be extraordinary. *Ab*normal even.

But can you imagine what you'd achieve? And how you'd feel? And the impact you'd have on the normal?

It's a mix of frightening and enlightening, but in the most beautiful way you could ever imagine.

Moreover, it's a mindset. A choice. It costs nothing.

So raise your glass and let's propose a toast:

'To the abnormal. To the happiness outliers. To those who dare. To those who are *THIIIIIS much* excited.

To YOU.

It's time to shine.'

Less sex in the city?

So, why don't we shine? If we all started out like Kian and life was *THIIIIIS much* exciting, where did it all go wrong? Why and when did life

> 'Some birds aren't meant to be caged. Their feathers are just too bright.'
>
> Arnold Bennett, 'Shawshank Redemption'

become a bit of a drag? Who or what extinguished the passion and pizzazz?

We suspect the modern world has a lot to answer for.

Humans are like an analogue receiver in a digital world. We have a multitude of TV channels and a dazzling array of social media, yet our attention is limited. Therefore, the only information that snags our attention is the truly exceptional 99.99th percentile. All day, every day, we're flooded with the truly extraordinary or excruciatingly mundane.

The internet sets clickbait traps, tempting you in because, come on, who doesn't want to know what their favourite soap star from the 1980s looks like now? You won't believe it, right? So you spend 20 minutes clodhopping through a maze of clickbait trash, accidentally clicking an advert or two on your way through the minefield, and the end result is, well, not quite as truly amazing as the headline said. *She looks kind of the same but a bit older.*

Meanwhile, 20 minutes of your life have ebbed away and you feel the need to go and have a shower to scrub away the stench of gullibility

The rest of the internet is the best of the best and the worst of the worst: cutest kittens, funniest jokes, biggest breasts. And our own lives seem a bit dull by comparison. My breasts are nothing to write home about, I can't tell a joke and, worse still, my cat is not clickworthy.

In an overcrowded marketplace there are two cool tricks guaranteed to lure readers. Firstly, choose a cool title (see above)

and second, chuck in a couple of quickies that will pique your readers' interest …

Did you know that men with a poor sense of smell have small willies? That's one of those niche facts that is just plain stunning. Chaps, not only is it true but it's something you'll remember and maybe mention next time you're in the pub with your mates. Chapesses, it's something you might mention to your other half when he's got a stuffy nose.

Secondly, and totally unrelated, I've just been reading an article by Ragnar Beer (Gottingen University) suggesting that the less sex you have, the more work you seek. Roll that one around in your head just for a moment. A rubbish sex life is associated with longer working hours?

Then allow yourself a furtive glance around the office. If Beer's correct, those who consistently stay late aren't getting any! Have a wry chuckle to yourself …

… and then the penny suddenly drops. *You're the one working stupid hours* and goddamit, Beer's spot on!

Beer's line of thinking is that if you're sexually deprived you need an outlet for your frustration, and one such outlet is more time in the office. I can see that this might be true, that those who work silly hours get less sex, but I'm not convinced about the causal direction. Do you work longer hours *because* there's no sex at home, or is there less sex at home *because* you work long hours? (For the record, we're both married to teachers, so sex is out of the question on a school night anyway.)

Putting the sex thing to one side, there's a deadly serious point about the long working hours culture that we've allowed ourselves to adopt. It's not just detrimental to your love life, but also to your productivity, health, longevity and happiness. Workaholism is like an internal time bomb, destroying relationships from the inside.

> 'Don't seek happiness. It's like an orgasm: if you over-think it, it goes away.'
>
> *Tim Minchin*

We're not arguing against the need for long hours. Sometimes. And in small bursts. The problem is that it's become 'always' and 'the norm'. If you think that sneaking off at 4pm is 'half a day', you're part of the problem.

Human beings are built to withstand stress. Indeed, stress is good for us. In small bursts, that is. The idea is that life trundles along, then something out of the ordinary happens, which, because of its novelty, causes us some anxiety. Our body/mind responds appropriately and we get over that particular hurdle, after which we return to 'normal'. We're the same as before but now we have a bit of extra learning. So the pattern we're built for is normal normal normal normal *stress* normal normal normal normal *stress* ...

The modern world has conspired against us and the pattern is far less of the normal and much more of the out of the ordinary. Thus, the pattern is stress stress stress stress *normal* stress stress stress ...

Stress is indeed the new black. There is far less downtime and our minds and bodies are living in a perpetual state of anxiety. There's a gradual build-up of the stress hormone cortisol. Back in the day, our active lifestyles helped clear cortisol out of the body. Nowadays, our sedentary existence allows it to build up. So, while stress in short bursts is good for you, our inability to rid our bodies of it causes chronic symptoms. It's not a feeling of permanent awfulness, more a background shrill of being hassled, drained, prickly or on edge.

That's the best-case scenario! It's easy to accelerate to anxiety, panic attacks and prolonged sadness. Sadly, 57 million anti-depressant prescriptions per year (in England alone) tell us that we've reached an unprecedented number of people who need meds to cope.

There aren't any laughs in that folks.

I'd like to write more but, got to dash, I can smell that someone's left a tap on next door. Gav, can you take over for a bit?

'That book'

My first book. I'm *THIIIIIS much* excited!

Isn't it fantastic how patiently a book will wait to be read?

And isn't SHINE a fabulous title? It has some wonderful connotations. As a verb, 'to shine' can mean to emit bright light or to be conspicuously competent. As a noun, 'a shine' is to have a sheen or lustre. Used in this context, it's nicely positioned at the sunnier end of 'rain or shine'.

It's also a liking or fancy, as in the phrase 'to take a shine to'.

All good. All desirable.

We've described how 'this book' came into being. But we don't want SHINE to be known as 'this book' – we'd much prefer it to be acknowledged as *'that book'*.

> 'That book changed my life.'
>
> 'That book made me wet myself.'
>
> 'That book was amazing.'
>
> 'That book revolutionized my thinking.'
>
> 'That book was like rocket fuel.'
>
> 'That book made me spend more time with my children.'
>
> 'That book made me re-evaluate my life.'
>
> 'That book shook my world.'

And yes, we appreciate there will be readers who say, *'That book was a totally over-hyped bag of shite.'*

Our aim is for more of the former but, hey, pleasing all of the people all of the time leads to our worst-case scenario, anodyne mediocrity.

'Boredom is the biggest disease in the world, darling.'

Freddie Mercury

In the same way that maths destroyed my love of numbers and science extinguished my love of cutting amphibians into small pieces, English destroyed my love of reading. Struggling through *A Midsummer Night's Dream* and making copious notes in the margins to highlight the sections that were *supposed* to be funny, that was a chore. I really enjoyed *Animal Farm*, a nice, easy read about some animals who organized themselves, and then BOOM, Mr Ely tells me it's not about pigs, sheep and horses at all. I'm like, 'Sir, the version that I read deffo was.'

My eyelids grew heavy as he regaled it as a tale of communism, capitalism and human greed.

Someone, somewhere has deemed the classics to be classic. Hence we're force-fed *Pride and Prejudice* and dictated to that *Of Mice and Men* is a must read. Ditto *To Kill a Mockingbird*. I get that *Mockingbird* might be a super read, but I gave up after Chapter 1 because it was a bag of shite.

In the art world, Da Vinci's 'Mona Lisa' is *'that painting'*. Priceless. It's the enigmatic smile apparently. And the guy with one ear. I forget his name. You know? The one who was crap at painting sunflowers? He's deemed to be a genius.

I've read plenty of decent books but *'that book'*, for me, is *The Hitchhiker's Guide to the Galaxy*, Douglas Adams' laugh-out-loud masterpiece – the book that restored my love of reading and, indeed, inspired me to have a go at writing. In 'THGttG' (as literally nobody is calling it), a person who can stay in control of virtually any situation is somebody who is said to know where his or her towel is, Adams' genius logic being that a towel has immense psychological value. If you pick up an intergalactic hitchhiker who has their towel with them, you will automatically assume that they are also in possession of a flannel, toothbrush, soap, tin of biscuits, flask, compass, map, gnat spray, wet-weather gear and so on. The towel gives you faith.

To bastardize a classic Kipling (poem, not a cake), if you can be in possession of your towel, when everyone around you has lost theirs, you are clearly someone to be reckoned with.

Think of SHINE as your intergalactic towel. Yes, the modern world is full-on crazy bonkers but when people see you carrying SHINE they will give you a second look, an admiring one.

'That book!' You are definitely someone to be reckoned with.

It ain't over 'til the fat man sings

And onto a story. SHINE is packed with them. Some might be funny, some quirky, some might even seem obscure. None are silly. Not even the silly ones.

Thailand – land of sunshine, beaches, sex tourism, lady boys and lazy racist stereotypes that we promised not to do. Oh, and more temples than you can shake a stick at (no, we're not sure what that means either, so we Googled it and guess what, even the internet doesn't know about the stick-shaking thing).

In one such temple, there's a 10-foot solid gold Buddha that attracts tourists with its shimmering glory. Next to it is a two-foot lump of clay that attracts nobody. Yet the exhibits are linked, with their story going back thousands of years …

True story. The original gold statue was housed in an ancient temple. The monks heard of a plot to raid the temple and loot it of its treasure, so they covered the gold Buddha with a thick cladding of clay, hoping the thieves would think it worthless.

It worked! Kind of. The thieves made off with a hoard of valuables but left the Buddha statue behind. Excellent! Along with a bloodbath of slaughtered monks. *Bummer.*

Then, in Indiana Jones times, a team of archaeologists cut a swathe through the jungle and came across the derelict and overgrown temple. They found the clay Buddha and thought it would look pretty cool in their museum, so they built a contraption, hoisted it onto their shoulders and struggled through the jungle. Remember, it was solid gold, so the men struggled. One of them collapsed in the heat and the statue fell, cracking the clay ever so slightly. That night, as they rested, the tropical rain lashed down and the next day, the team awoke to a glint of gold. The torrential rain had washed away some of the clay, revealing the 24-carat truth.

And we can't help thinking that's a nice way to anchor our first chapter. The bleedin' obvious point being that we're all a bit like that Buddha. No, no, not literally pot-bellied and cross-legged, but *metaphorically* – as in, we accumulate layers. We learn the rules of life. Work hard, be a decent friend, have a social life, get noticed at work, earn more cash, don't swear in front of the kids …

Layer upon layer is added until our shine gets diminished. Look here, loyal reader, we're not alchemists. We don't need to be. There's gold inside folks, but the outside can become a bit heavy and dull. We want to chip away at the crusty stuff so you can tackle life in all your golden glory.

Chipping away is a crucial concept. Most books are 'additive', giving you theories, principles and concepts to remember and apply. In the past you might, for example, have had to learn and remember seven habits, five levels, ten commandments, eight laws or twelve principles. These are the layers in the Buddha story. You can accumulate a lot of shit.

We love you. You've gone to the trouble of buying our book so, as a big fat thank you, we will treat you to some 'subtractive psychology'. Less is more. Let's help take some shit off you. We want to give you *less* to think about, *less* to do and take things *off* your mind. Possibly, heaven forbid, take yourself and life *less* seriously.

Ask yourself, all those years of 'doing more' – those seven habits, five levels, ten commandments, eight laws and twelve principles. Has it worked? Have you found happiness? Or clarity? Or is life just full-on exhausting?

All your worldly problems may seem complicated. But what if they're not? What if they can all be solved with some insight, wrapped in a fluffy down-feathered duvet of simplicity?

Wouldn't that make a nice change?

We all have this great inner psychological inertia. This is because our minds are essentially accumulations of habits. We all have physical habits, like brushing our teeth or flossing the cat. But we also have mental habits – biases and stereotypes we regularly fall back upon. These are worn and weathered explanations for the world's difficulties, assumptions that get us out of a psychological pickle. We rely on these mental habits just as we rely on physical habits – they sort and rearrange the world for us without us having to expend any conscious effort.

> 'Fate rarely calls upon us at the moment of our choosing.'
>
> *Optimus Prime, Leader of the Autobots*

By the time we're old enough to enter the workplace, we have developed into emotional, walking, talking, lumbering habit machines. We've developed a sense of who we are and what we're good and bad at. Most functioning adults also have a canny knack of being able to imagine how others perceive us, which gives rise to a whole load of issues around self-consciousness and embarrassment. In short, we all end up with an identity. If you want to change 'who you are' in the truest personal development sense of 'leaning into being your best self', then it's worth analogizing that life's not a nippy speedboat zipping about on a millpond sea – you're carrying a lifetime of emotional and psychological cargo and hauling it across the vast oceans of your unconscious.

We want to provide you with some quick wins, but a lot of personal change takes time, courage and practice, so please expect a lot of sloshing around.

Casper and the vol-au-vents

The human brain is capable, and generally very good at, making maps of time. That means we can remember the past, compare it to the present and imagine the future. The upside of this ability is that we can reflect and learn in a proactive way, we can design systems to deal with our environment, we can anticipate changing seasons and be ready for them, we can make plans for the future. The downside is that we can be haunted by our past or paralysed by a fearful future. We can end up dreading change. Other animals don't have this thinking capacity.

I can't prove that last sentence, it's just a hunch. I am not an ant-eater so don't actually know what goes on in its mind. Ant-eaters may, in fact, be merrily reminiscing about the good old days when ants were in plentiful supply, back in the summer of 1974.

And after a hearty ant meal they might dream of moving onto pastures new, where the ants are bigger and the days warmer. But it's unlikely. They're more likely to have their noses in small holes, extending their sticky tongues until their brain sends a primitive signal saying their bellies are full of ants. Then they'll sleep, shit and start again.

Excuse the clunky metaphor, but you and I know people who are living the ant-eater life.

Of course, there's a host of valid reasons that we fall into work/ eat/shit/sleep/repeat mode. There's a snappy Bilbo Baggins' quote – 'I feel thin, sort of stretched, like butter scraped over too much bread' – that we think reveals a profound truth of the modern era. 'Busyness' is a contemporary disease that it's difficult to shake off.

Have you noticed the new default response to, 'Hi there, how you doin'?' is, 'Oh, you know, keeping busy.'

> 'So much time, and so little to do! Strike that, reverse it.'
>
> *Willy Wonka*

And there are levels of busy. I've heard people say they are crazily busy or, more correctly, stupidly busy. Life has become a bit like the wonderful German word, *Schilderwald*: a street with so many road signs that you become lost.

I doubt anyone really wants to live a harried and stressed life crammed with busyness. Bursts of busy, for sure. But full-on, relentless, jam-packed, bonkers busy? Is it *really* better than the opposite? Is exhausted and dead on your feet better than refreshed with a spring in your step?

How did we get here, rushing along the platform of busyness central?

It's something we collectively force one another to do. It's copying. It's interesting

> 'This morning I went to a meeting of my premature ejaculators' support group. But it turns out that it's tomorrow.'
>
> *Gary Delaney*

to dare ask yourself: what are you busy doing? If you're busy doing back-to-back shifts at the paediatric intensive care unit, then our metaphorical caps are doffed. But if you're busy sitting in traffic, back-to-back meetings and scrolling your smartphone, our caps remain undoffed and our eyebrows raised in a head-teachery glare.

It might be that you've become addicted to busyness and dread the alternative – unadulterated peace and quiet. Time with yourself. Think about it, if your diary is crammed with so much stuff that stopping for a wee at the motorway services causes your day to fall out of kilter, then that's a nod to how busy and important you must be. If you're in such demand at so many meetings that you're consistently arriving harried and just a little bit late then, crikey, you must have significance. If you're struggling to attend your children's Christmas play because of work commitments then, goodness me, your job must be important. If you've got to set the alarm for 5.30am to catch the early train to London then, holy cow, that must be a crucial meeting. If you slump through your front door, say a cursory '*Hi*' to your family before dashing upstairs to log onto your emails, boy are you important. If you sit in bed, next to your wonderful partner, scrolling through Twitter, then you must have so many followers …

Jeez. How important are you? All these people need you!

The question we've not quite been daring enough to ask is: what if all this busyness stuff is a ruse? What if we're just papering over the cracks of meaninglessness?

In the Baggins quote, most individuals and organizations complain of not having enough butter – *it's not fair, we need more resources, more time and more staff to get the job done*.

It's unfair! One nob of butter can't possibly cover the whole loaf.

But what if we came at it from a different angle? What would happen if, instead of always seeking more butter, we found the discipline to cover less bread? This might sound harsh, but in the interests of genuinely challenging your thinking, what if spreading our butter too thin is a form of hiding? It helps us to be busy because it makes it unlikely we will have an impact.

The refreshing reality is that we're not going to give you any more stuff to do. *Phew!* You will be delighted to know that we're on your side – we reckon you're already doing more than your fair share. Your life is full-on. Your workplace head count has been butchered to the point that you're doing the work of three people. You are ruthlessly efficient to the point that you've adopted the email Russian Doll system, whereby your little yellow folders have little yellow folders inside them.

We think that modernity has converted too many of us from 'human beings' into 'human doings', where your burgeoning to-do list has become so overwhelming that you might have forgotten who you are. So, in a refreshing deviation from the norm, we are not going to give you anything to do, but we are going to challenge who you're *being*. If you let that sink in for a moment, you will realize it's a 'yikes' moment. Because this doesn't merely challenge your working hours, but your home life too.

If you come on our workshops, you'll hear us banging on about the average lifespan of 4000 weeks. Is that a big number? It's interesting that if you announce it to a bunch of primary schoolchildren they'll leap around the hall in delight, whereas an adult audience will absorb the same data with a raised eyebrow and a look of mild panic. *Really? Is that true? It's not a very big number. I've used a few!*

'The trouble is, you think you have time.'

Buddha

The simple truth is not only simple and true, but deadly so. And it's this, something that I cottoned onto a couple of years ago: *everywhere I go, I'm there* (told you it was deadly simple).

What I mean is that for the entirety of my lifetime, I'm stuck with me for the entire 4000-week gig. I can run as fast as I like, but there's not a single second of escape from me.

And you're stuck with you.

So, if I'm stuck with myself for 4000 weeks, I may as well be stuck with a version of me that I'm proud of. A me that shines. A version of myself with something about him: energy, vigour, zest, happiness, positivity, confidence and passion. Rather than the rather worn-out, insipid version of me that I hung around with for my first 35 years.

The dirty little truth is that if I want to be the awesome version of me, I need to 'do less' and 'be more'. In a spooky twist of the universe, by being more of yourself at your best, you will accidentally get more done. Moreover, you will have bags more energy to devote to things outside of work. Indeed, you might even have stumbled on one of the secrets of happiness, namely that if there's a revolution to be started, it has to start inside your head first.

The outside-in nature of thought has fooled us into thinking that 'I am me' in this body in this time called 'life'. Therefore I'd better climb as high as the corporate ladder will take me, score as many points and accumulate as much stuff as I can before I die. These trappings of 'success' and 'materialism' are sadly mistaken for signs of accomplishment on the 4000-week journey. You have succeeded so long as you get promoted and have loads of stuff.

Yet we don't often see a tombstone with 'Here lies Brenda. She was a senior manager and, boy, did she have loads of stuff'. Invariably the engravings are more about your qualities and what your life meant to those left behind. This works on a family level and on a work level.

So, in order to focus your mind, let's skip ahead to the end of your 4000 weeks. Cutting to the chase, there's going to be a bit of a do. With some sandwiches. Yes folks, church is a great place for the 'hatch' and 'match' parts of life, but the 'dispatch' bit can be more gruelling. Your family and friends will gather, with a pervading sense of sobriety, to talk about you. Indeed, you will be the sole topic of conversation for the entire day.

We're hoping they will be proud of what you've done, but that's not going to be what they talk about. They will be reminiscing about who you've been. Hence, the kind of person you are becomes crucial.

So here are two killer questions. We project you to that fateful day, to the moment you've been dispatched and the party moves to the sandwiches and cup of tea bit – you're allowed to be there in spirit. And if you hover, Casper-like, near the vol-au-vents and listen in, what kind of conversations would you like people to be having? What kind of memories do you want them to be recalling?

Herein lies your true power. If you shine during your 4000 weeks, you will not only enjoy a radiant life, you will also enable others to shine and stand a pretty good chance of lighting up your own funeral.

Chapter 2

A RACE TO THE BOTTOM?

Time to get your SHINE on!

In which we start a bit ETish before having a pop at pop culture. We wouldn't want to be without wi-fi but we argue that social media and saturated news coverage have become weapons of mass distraction, causing massive social destruction. The rise and rise of the 'e-personality' is likened to Harry Potter's invisibility cloak, and we sneak in a really clever Dr Jekyll pun before giving you permission to 'invoke your 25th'.

We've devoted the whole of Chapter 7 to 'real stress' but, for now, please keep an open mind while we regale you with stories of self-inflicted stress. And remember, to double-quote Stan from 'South Park', 'dude, this is pretty fucked up, right here'. And 'just because we laugh doesn't mean we don't care'.

Finishing with the unlikeliest of shifts, from 'Blue Monday' to 'Gérard Depardieu Monday', Chapter 2 proves to be a whole lot cleverer than it looks.

Confused? Excellent.

Off we trot …

Phone a friend

Some drink from the fountain of knowledge. Others gargle. Some are knowledge tee-total.

Andy's a proper guzzler. He describes himself as a recovering academic. He's thinking of starting 'Academics Anonymous' where a bunch of elbow-patched boffins would sit in a circle and take turns standing up and saying 'Hi, I'm so-and-so from Durham. And I've got a problem …'.

You wouldn't have to dig too far to discover that so-and-so from Cambridge, Bristol, St Andrews and York have all got the same problem – deliberate obfuscation and Daedalianizing. *Doh! There I go again!* What I meant to say was that academics are really good at finding complicated ways to say things and even better at not really saying what they mean.

Academic papers are littered with hedging adverbs, like arguably, plausibly and questionably, as if adding an '-ably' to as many words as possible renders them harmless. Mary Aiken calls it 'sleight of word', a career-protection mechanism, just in case, at some point in time, an idea might be proven wrong.

No sleight of word from us. No fence sitting either. Here's how it is.

I've got 30 emails sitting at the bottom of my inbox. They've been there since 2013 and I'm beginning to think I might not get round to them. You're the same.

Mobile communications were introduced as a tool for freedom. The 1990s were heady days because, for the first time in the history of human kind, you could access information from anywhere, at any time. *The entire world is on your phone. Woohoo!*

Insidiously, the freedom tool has become your captor. You're now available 24/7 and therefore trapped in a loop of 'phoney productivity'. *The entire world is on your phone. Oh shit!*

We're both old enough (Andy in particular) to remember what it was like to have no smartphone. In fact, any mobile phone. And it was bliss. Andy remembers watching 'Dallas' in the 1980s and JR was phoning Bobby on this brick of a thing, with a chuffing great aerial, and thinking *Those 'cellphones', they'll never catch on.*

At a talk recently, 'young Gav' was discussing this very topic with a crowd of 13-year-olds. Gav mentioned that he remembers not having a mobile phone. The entire room burst out laughing. The following conversation ensued…

Girl: 'But how did you speak to your friends?'

Gav: 'You walked to their house. Or cycled.'

Laughter

Girl: [puzzled expression] 'What if they lived in the next town?'

Gav: 'You walked to their house. Or you cycled.'

More laughter

Girl: [getting exasperated] 'What if they live too faaaar for that?'

Gav: 'You picked up the house phone.'

A moment's silence from the kids while they looked at each other

29

Girl: 'What's a "house phone"?'

Gav: 'You know. The phone you have at home that sits halfway up the stairs and no one uses but your parents still pay for it anyway?'

Laughter

Girl: 'But what if they lived in another country and it was too expensive to call?'

Gav: 'You wrote a letter. And posted it.' [starting to feel silly]

Peals of laughter

Girl: 'What if you were out seeing friends and you weren't going to make it home at the time your mum said you needed to be home by?'

Gav: 'You found a phone box and reversed the charges. If your mum accepted the call you were fine. If she didn't you were in trouble.'

Silence. Furrowed brows

Gav: 'Reversing the charges? Anyone?'

Silence. Shrugging. Kids start to become disinterested because nearly 40-year-old Gav's a relic from times gone by. They reach for their mobiles to check for fresh cat pictures on Instagram.

A Nottingham Trent University study found that Brits check their phones 85 times a day, and more than one-third of 15-year-old children in the UK are classified as 'extreme internet users', defined as those who are online for more than six hours daily outside of school. Bizarrely, only Chilean children reported more.

Six hours a day, seven days a week equates to 91 days per year, *spent on your phone.*

You might have a smartphone, but that's not a very smart statistic. In fact, it's a stupid and sad one. Maybe we should rebrand them as stupid phones? Or take the learning from cigarette packaging but, instead of tumours, phones could carry pictures of a zombie apocalypse.

We're in the midst of mass human migration to cyber-space or, as clinical psychologist Michael Seto says, 'We are living through the largest unregulated social experiment of all time – a generation of youth who have been exposed to extreme content online.'

What will happen to this generation? Who knows? Simon Sinek argues that there is already a generation of young people entering the workplace who've never had to do anything hard or struggle. Disparagingly nicknamed the snowflake generation, these are the kids for whom everyone got a medal at sports day. Andy's son has a mercy law in rugby whereby if you're getting thrashed, you end the game because nobody wants their feelings hurt. Devil's advocate, just for a sec – what if having your feelings hurt makes you stronger and inspires you to train harder, so a few good thumpings mean your team emerges stronger?

Rhetorically, have we raised a generation of 'safe 'n' easy'? When was the last time your kids climbed a tree or swam in a reservoir? Playgrounds have woodchips and soft play areas. We wear cycle helmets. Our meds have child-proof lids. We're cosseted. Is life too easy? Too safe?

Andy spent the entire summer of 1977 with scabbed knees and friction burns on his outer thighs. They were medals of honour from falling off his bike or doing slide tackles in six-hour games of football. Six weeks of scabs. Mostly, the scabs had scabs.

This is not some heroic call to arms to throw our children, naked, into big patches of nettles or force them to swim a river to prove their worth. This is not North Korea. Neither is it an attempt to say that the good old days were indeed the good old days.

We're merely hinting that technology and the modern rules of life have solved old problems by giving us new psychological and social ones.

In her marvelous (and terrifying) book, *The Cyber Effect*, Mary Aiken tells us what we already sense, that when we're online we develop an impaired sense of judgement – the cyber effect – the $E = MC^2$ of the twenty-first century.

Your online persona is the real-world equivalent of Harry Potter's invisibility cloak. Once unseen you become imbued with magical powers, aka the 'online disinhibition effect' (ODE). Individuals are bolder, less inhibited and more confident. In related news, psychologists have reported on the rise of the 'e-personality', your online presence that amplifies the self-centred nature of human beings. This has led to an 'epidemic of narcissism' that manifests in a disinterest in the lives of others.

With empathy on the decline and the '*me me me*' yelp of narcissism on the rise, there's a dark side brewing. There's an awful lot of awfulness, online bile spitting, Twitter death threats, cyber bullying and trolling. Once cloaked you can say what you like to whomever you like. You can cause huge upset by saying poisonous things from under the cloak of invisibility that you'd never dream of saying to someone's face. Because in the flesh and blood world, you're a nice person, right?

All of the above can become rather scary and, if you'll excuse our all-too-clever pun, rather like a big game of Jekyll and Hide.

> ### Definition
>
> 'Slacktivism: where people delude themselves that signing an online petition or retweeting a message is a form of social action, when the reality is that you haven't moved from your seat.'

All this gives rise to quite a big 'so what'?

We are social animals, wired to connect. In fact, we have to connect with other human beings otherwise we become isolated and depressed. Humans have developed an 'empathy circuit' in our brains, which, if damaged, can curtail our ability to understand what others are feeling. Evolutionary biologists have shown we are social animals who have naturally evolved to be empathic and cooperative, just like our primate cousins. And child psychologists have revealed that even three-year-olds are able to step outside themselves and see other people's perspectives. It is now evident that we have an empathic side to our natures that is just as strong as our selfish inner drives.

Richard Layard advocates 'deliberate cultivation of the primitive instinct of empathy' because 'if you care more about other people relative to yourself, you are more likely to be happy.'

Plain and simple: empathy is the *cornerstone of good relationships* and good relationships are the *cornerstone of happiness*.

Is the modern world killing empathy? Cyberspace is a distinct place. You may be accessing it from a familiar environment, like the comfort of your own home, but as soon as you go online you have travelled to a different location in terms of your awareness or consciousness, your emotions, your responses and your behaviour. Your body might be in the room, but you aren't. Remember when we sat down on a Saturday night as a family to watch TV? Together. We'd laugh together, chat together, eat together, share together. Compare this to the modern Saturday night experience. We all sit down together to watch TV on our phones, laptops and tablets. Several screens all on the go at the same time. We don't laugh at the same time anymore, we don't chat anymore, we don't share the moment anymore. That's too strong. It's not that we don't do those things, but that we do them much less often.

Ditto mealtimes. How many of you are guilty of sitting down at mealtimes and everyone is on their phone? Do you even notice what you're eating? Are you paying attention to each other? If you're with your family or out with friends, why do you even need a phone?

More and more now we see parents with their children eating in restaurants and the kids get handed phones or tablets. It's so sad when you see mum and dad on their phones and the child sits staring into space with no one to talk to.

How many of us lie in bed with our partners at the end of a day, in silence, zero chat because we're staring at our phones? How many of us wake up in the morning and the first thing we do is reach for the phone? It's like a drug. We need that hit in the morning.

Economics has a phrase, 'opportunity cost', a wonderful way of getting you to think about the price of the next best alternative. A teenager, for example: if they spend eight hours a day engaging in extreme internet use, that's eight hours that they could have been doing something else. Just to ram the point home, eight hours is a third of your day (or half of the awake part of it). It's the academic equivalent of Jim Bowen's fabulous 1970s catchphrase: 'Look at what you could have won'.

> 'I've worked with hundreds of heroin addicts and crystal meth addicts, and what I can say is that it's easier to treat a heroin addict than a true screen addict.'
>
> Dr Nicholas Kardaras, author of Glow Kids

Everything you ever do has an opportunity cost. Time has an opportunity cost. Reading this book has an opportunity cost. You could have been emptying the dishwasher or cleaning the toilet instead. Hence, what a fabulous choice you're making.

Nick Carr warns that email and social media cause people to become addicted to 'mindlessly pressing levers in the hope of receiving a pellet of social or intellectual nourishment'. We think it might be even bigger than that. The problem with an infinite inbox and dazzling menu of social media is that these are hours that you are not going to get back. They cost time. These hours have an opportunity cost. You are not reading a book to your child, playing with your toddler on the floor, chatting with your family at the dinner table, talking with your partner before bed. When you are checking your phone or spending time surfing websites, you are effectively in a different environment. You have gone somewhere else. You are not present in real-world terms.

Look, we're not all high and mighty. We both do the social media thing. Just be aware, it's costing your life. That's a mighty big price tag, so might it be worth investing chunks of time elsewhere?

Invoking your 25th

I've recently come to the conclusion that 24 hours just isn't enough. I'd like to suggest that we add an extra one but that it's not fixed, it's a floater. (So to speak, man gag probably.)

To keep it simple, it becomes known as 'the 25th' and it comes with three rules:

1. The 25th hour is available to everyone.
2. You can use it at any time, but only once a week.
3. You're not allowed to get angry when someone else plays their 25th.

Here's how it works. Some might use it early doors. The alarm scares you into another dark morning, but you can roll over, hit snooze, text your workplace, 'Invoking my 25th' and go back to sleep for an hour. Or you get home from work, knackered, to a kitchen full of dirty pots that your teenagers couldn't be bothered to clear up. You've got a dishwasher to empty, meals to prepare but, nope, you yell, 'Invoking my 25th' as you retire to the lounge, feet up, gorging on last night's 'Love Island', with a cuppa.

Nobody's allowed to meddle with your 25th. You have complete freedom to use it in any way you wish. Your boss demands your PowerPoint presentation, right now? Playing your 25th gives you an extra hour. It's Saturday afternoon and your wife decides that, 'We should go and look at flooring' ... and, all of a sudden, you begin to see the wonder of the 25th.

The beauty is that by slowing down, you force everyone else into slowing down too. The meeting can't start without you. The family meal can't start without you. We're not allowed to get angry, so everyone has to chill. We learn to wait. Your extra hour gives everyone else an extra hour too.

Flawless.

What would you do with yours?

Who you gonna call? *Stress Busters!*

The self-awareness onion means that as you peel back the layers, it can get a bit teary. We appreciate that modern life can be harsh and unwavering in its full-on-ness. There are times when events will knock you sideways and backwards. In fact, you'll be floored several times and getting back into the ring seems beyond you.

We have a chapter in waiting for those times.

This section is for all the other times. The days when you accidently collude with the modern world and become a conjurer of bad news, creating a whole load of problems out of thin air. 'And for my next trick, here's an empty hat. See? Nothing in it. And with a tap of my magic wand, whoosh, I pull out a big, fat, hairy, buck-toothed problem. Ta-Daaa!'

[The audience swoons. *Magicking shit out of nothing? That's an impressive trick.*]

Example. Here is the national news …

> Bad shit is happening in the world. Your politicians are bent. People are dying. There's not enough money to keep society ticking over. Poor people are still poor. There are wars and famines. There's an earthquake somewhere you once went to on holiday. There's terrible weather. Brexit rumbles on. There's some sort of inquiry into some shit that happened a long time ago. Someone's gone and blown themselves up and, oh look, there's a celebrity divorce thing happening …

And now the news in your area … all the above, but slightly less bad.

> There's some crime and a local company has announced some job losses. The trains are shit. Here are some angry people complaining about something or other. It's not raining at the moment, but there's plenty on the way. Thanks for listening, now back to the studio for the main headlines again …
>
> Bad shit is happening in the world. Your politicians are bent. People are dying. There's not enough money to keep society ticking over. Poor people …

This is piped into your home 24/7. Nowadays it's more than just news. I've heard it called 'outrage porn' – rather than report on real stories and real issues the media find it easier (and more profitable) to find something mildly offensive, broadcast it to a wide audience to create outrage, and then broadcast that outrage back across the population in a way that creates more outrage. You can go online and comment on the news. You can # and contribute to the debate. So the news is not the news. The news is the outrage that the news causes. It's our teenage wizard again, but in a new title: *Harry Potter and the Chamber of Outrage.*

So, sucker punch number one: we think some people have got addicted to feeling offended. It's the high and mighty moral ground because, if I'm offended, that means my values are better than yours. That might be true. Who knows? But by taking things slightly less seriously and choosing not to be offended, you'll feel a ton happier.

Which leads us into a solar plexus punch of point number two: *just because you're offended, it doesn't mean you're right.*

We've been chopping away at how wrong we are and, as a result, we're becoming less and less wrong every day. And less angry and offended. We have a sneaky feeling that 500 years down the line they'll be looking back at this time in history and laughing uproariously at how we let money and jobs define our lives – how we heaped praise on public figures but forgot to praise the real heroes in our lives.

And below the belt thump number three: we're firm believers that there is such a thing as 'good stress'. Technically, it's called 'eustress', where you're challenged in just the right way. This kind of stress enables you to grow and learn. Indeed, it can put you under pressure to perform, which leads you to up your game to the level of greatness.

This kind of stress is akin to a footballer giving 120%. For many a year, Andy would shake his fist at the TV as the goal scorer was interviewed and would trot out the cliché that he's given 120%. You and I, we're educated people, we know that you *cannot give 120%.*

But if humble pie had calories, I'd be as fat as Simple Simon. The footballers have been right all along, because you can give 120% if you've achieved something that you didn't think was possible. And good stress stretches you that extra bit, beyond what you'd thought possible, hence our word 'greatness', your new personal best.

We believe that there is another side to stress. One that is complete nonsense. Stress that, as if by magic, you've conjured in your own head.

There are types of people that fall into this category: those who know they are doing it and those who don't. Those who know they are doing it don't just know they are doing it, they love it. Have you ever worked with someone who *loves* creating moments of drama and stress? Everything's a 'nightmare'. Crikey, they're hard work!

However, we're not going to waste ink on them, we'd rather introduce you to fake stress that's created accidentally, through habits of thinking.

Here are some examples, and some stress-busting ideas. Please note, just because they're funny doesn't mean they're *actually* funny.

Example one: putting fuel in your car can be stressful. For those who choose it, that is. We wonder how many of you have done that thing where you put £20 worth of fuel in your car …

… and one penny!

What do many of us do in this situation? We top it up! By £9.99! Many people would rather spend an extra £9.99 just so that we have a nice round number to look at.

We like to encourage a bit of positive deviance so, next time you're filling up, put in the most random amount of fuel you can. We recommend £14.61, or £36.11. Look at the cashier's face, they might not be able to cope. Gav witnessed a woman doing this recently. He knew she was gunning for £30 because she'd stopped at £29.95 for a breather. She composed herself for the final 5p push. A quick flick of the petrol gun and she jumped to £29.97. Gav had stopped filling his own car. He was mesmerized. The pressure!

Flick again. £29.99! No way! Everyone knows you can't do a penny, not in the modern era. Gav was willing her on as she shaped to give it a go.

£30 and 4p!

That's a jump of 5p. A disappointing end. Amateurish even. She was angry with herself. But the game wasn't over, Gav watched slack-jawed, as she played on, for £40. Missing again, she audibly cursed herself.

Gav turned his attention back to his own fuel. He'd decided to go for £42.49. He'd bloody well show her that randomness was much more fun. He began his own refuelling and, as the gauge ticked through the low numbers, he dared a glance at the lady. He relaxed. She'd hit £50, square on.

Gav walked away, eyebrow raised knowingly at the cashier's wavery voice as he'd declared, 'Pump number 5' and she'd replied, '£42.49?', hesitantly, almost questioningly, because nobody had ever paid that amount before. As he moseyed back to his car as only a true pump gunslinger can, he considered the woman's plight. In her pursuit of a perfectly round number, not only had she spent £20 more than she wanted, she'd also managed to curse and get angry. All in all, a needless three minutes. Ridiculous in fact. Definitely a case of fake stress.

We refer to her as 'one of them'. 'Them' who have several of those three-minute episodes carved into their day. 'Them' who might even have a few five or ten-minute extended moments, with an occasional half hour prolonged stretch of tutting. In fact, she'll be one of 'them' who, by the end of their day, has spent hours in a self-generated state of anger, irritation, frustration and annoyance by something or someone or some minor situation that JUST DOESN'T MATTER.

But we want you to think about how YOU react to these moments. As we all know, the real secret to finding out how you react to Fake Stress™ lies, of course, with Example two: your toilet-roll holders at home. Bear with us on this one.

Think about your toilet-roll holder. If you don't have a toilet-roll holder, then *imagine* you have a toilet-roll holder and stop putting your loo roll on the radiator! 'But it keeps it warm,' we hear you shout.

Weirdo.

Imagine a cardboard tube on your toilet-roll holder. Many of you reading this will already be getting frustrated because in your mind, 'someone else should've changed it'. There's a simple way to dissipate this anger – get over it and just change it yourself.

> 'A soulmate is someone who appreciates your level of weird.'
>
> Bill Murray

Now imagine yourself replacing it. Now that you've replaced it, have a good think. Does your toilet roll hang over and away from the wall? Or under?

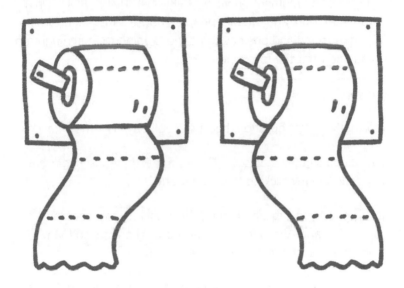

These are questions we've asked on many occasions at conferences around the world and it's amazing how many people put their hands up to the first question in such a way that suggests, 'AND THERE IS NO OTHER WAY!'

The fact that some of you even have a 'correct' way is a cause for concern. Yes, dear reader, in a bizarre twist of emotional contagion, your obsession for having a preferred way to hang your toilet roll is actually causing your author tag team to sweat.

Of course, there's *always* another way to do something. Like your job. Or life. You might not like it. You might not be used to it. It might be uncomfortable. But there is *always* another way.

We got to our point through toilet roll, but we got there!

We'd love you to put this to the test for us. Everywhere you go in life from this moment onwards, TURN THE TOILET ROLL. Do it at home, at work and in other people's houses. Just keep turning toilet rolls round and one day someone is going to march right up to you and utter the following words:

'Is it you?'

And that's a great question, because you'll say, 'Is it me what?'

And of course they then say it like it's a real thing: 'Is it you that keeps turning my fucking toilet roll round?'

At this point you can stand there, think back to this book and realize: Gav and Andy are absolutely right. There are so many things that just shouldn't be stressful. EVER.

But we let them be. We allow them to be. In fact, we don't just allow them to be, we choose them to be.

Point of fact – the only time you should ever be stressed about toilet roll is if there is *no* toilet roll.

Our petrol and loo roll examples are mere snowflakes on the tip of the tutting iceberg. We wonder how many things there are in your job that stress you out, annoy or frustrate you? The modern world is like a Victorian sewage pipe, clogged with fake stress, the vast majority of which is created by the people who work there.

Paradox time. The biggest problem every workplace has is the people that work there. And yet, the biggest solution every workplace has is the people that work there.

What these incredibly high performing, hugely successful organizations have are these incredible individuals, who can pull together. Who can cut through all the bullshit, all the nonsense and get back to the why, the purpose, the reason the organization existed in the first place. And when that happens, our people shine.

Although we're a writing tag team, sometimes one of us has to just sit back and admire the words that the other has created Andy can now put his feet up and wipe away a tear, while Gav articulates what Andy's been trying to be say in his previous four books …

When you SHINE, others SHINE. You attract other SHINERS. It's infectious. You have rays of light coming out of your face that light up the whole fucking sky like the Batman signal and we all just find each other. It's a call. Commissioner Gordon would be jealous.

Batman was used as a weapon of psychological intimidation on the numerous criminals of Gotham City. Your SHINE is so much more than that. When you SHINE you are a weapon: of psychological encouragement. A weapon of comfort and empowerment. In fact, you're the opposite of a weapon; something or someone who brings peace or heals people. You heal yourself with happiness. Awesomeness. With magic powers that only you have. Your SHINE is a medicine. A shield of joy. Protect and serve yourself for a change. SHINE.

Fake stress is everywhere, it fills our lives right up to the brim and we need to consciously make choices to reduce the amount of it we experience. The clue's in the name. It's fucking fake. It's not real. You've manufactured it.

Example? Here's the ultimate fake stress, the biggest myxoma toxic rabbit that humans have ever pulled out of their own hat: Blue Monday.

It's the name given to a day in January (typically the third Monday of the month) claimed to be the most depressing day of the year. This was calculated using many factors, including weather conditions, debt level, time since Christmas, time since failing our New Year's resolutions, low motivational levels, *blah blah*.

And now Blue Monday is a thing. It's recognized as 'officially the most depressing day of the year', AN ACTUAL THING THAT PEOPLE BELIEVE IN. People buy into it.

So, our response … what utter nonsense.

Note, there is no equivalent happy day. Nobody has designated, say, 14 March as the day that you wake up and it's light outside, the birds are chirping, the weather warming and therefore designated as the most joyful day of the year. Crappy day, yes. Happy day, no.

Here's why Blue Monday is bollocks.

Blue Monday was created, invented, made up in 2005 as part of a marketing campaign for a travel company to convince people like you and me to part with our cash to buy holidays.

There is zero science out there to back the idea of Blue Monday. It comes as no surprise that mental health charities are doing their bit to fight back against Blue Monday and coming up with their own ways of doing something far nicer. We know of one charity that has been hosting Brew Monday. On the third Monday of every January they open up their centres and invite people in to see first hand the wonderful work they are doing for people with depression. What a fantastic spin on what is an incredibly negative idea.

We've been thinking about things we can all be doing moving forward, because you know next time Blue Monday comes around you're going to go into work and you're going to meet those people who will actually say things like, 'Aww it's Blue Monday, I feel really down'. You'll know these people, they use things like this as an excuse just to be miserable and critical.

So, let's spin this around.

We could quite simply just change it to *'Do Monday'*, and kick its ass! We could have *'To-Do Monday'*, where as a team you agree that by the end of Monday, the first day of the working week, you've collectively smashed your entire week's to do list. What a great, positive and productive way to approach your working week!

Instead of Blue Monday, how about *'Balloo Monday'* when you surprise your team by coming to work dressed as a bear.

Or *'Shoe Monday'*? Everyone must wear the craziest, brightest, shiniest, most glittery pair of footwear they can. Make it an annual thing, at the very least it's going to put a great big smile on people's faces.

It's just about finding something different other than Blue Monday.

'Stew Monday'. Spend your Sunday creating and making something delicious and on the Monday everyone brings something in and an almighty stew picnic ensues!

'Fondue Monday'; same principle but with cheese instead of stew. *'Caribou Monday'*; same again, but the ingredients

might be more difficult to source. Maybe just turn up in antlers instead.

'*Gérard Depardieu Monday*'? Everyone wears big noses and speaks French. Yes, we might have stretched a good idea too far, but the point is that you don't have to fall for a big, fat misery con. We challenge you to look forward to Blue Monday, and do the opposite. Make it a '*Woohoo Monday*'.

But the problem doesn't end there. Let's be honest, the idea of the dreaded Monday morning doesn't really just sit within a single Monday does it? In fact, it creeps into our weekends.

We've all heard the phrase 'Sunday Blues'. Some call it the 'Sunday Sads' or 'Smonday', the exact point that you start hating Sunday because Monday comes next.

There have been many studies into the subject of work fear. Apparently there is a proper name for it, Dimanchophobia. The *Huffington Post* reported a study for the Monster jobs site stating that 78% of those who took part in the study said they suffer from the Sunday Blues.

So 78% of us lose a day or at least a big chunk of their day to dread, fear, anxiety – the list goes on. Surely rocking your Monday is way more appealing than dreading your Monday? It's remarkably easy to argue it the other way – that Fridays are a disaster. Friday is another week closer to death, yet we rejoice on a collective #TGIFriday

Top death tip:

Try to think of death as the long vacation you've been needing.

We've given you a few suggestions to replace Blue Monday; why not make every Monday a day to inspire? Kick your week off in style. A day to imagine, create and innovate. And you don't have to come up with 52 different themes that rhyme with Blue! But if you do, then be sure to share them with us!

We love Mondays. *No, we really do*. Monday is your chance to get up and start the week the way you mean to go on. You *need* to get up, so if you're going to rise then you might as well shine.

Bright.

Chapter 3

A SPOONFUL OF SUGAR

Mary Poppins vs Mr Banks

In which there is no introduction, as such. Just this …

Think of the best albums you've ever bought (clarification for the under 30s, an 'album' was an entire collection of a dozen or so songs that a band released. You'd buy them all. Yes, even the bad ones) – track one was always the best, right? Nearly all bands will put their hit singles up front.

No band in the history of music has ever put their best song as track three. Like ever. That'd be potty. Track three's where you hide stuff. It's a non-single. A B-side, at best.

We are not 'all bands ever'. Welcome to Chapter 3 …

Hail Mary

> 'A person who has good thoughts cannot ever be ugly. You can have a wonky nose and a crooked mouth and a double chin and stick-out teeth, but if you have good thoughts they will shine out of your face like sunbeams and you will always look lovely.'
>
> *Roald Dahl*

When I (Gav) was 18 years old, I left home and went to uni, where I spent four years training to become a primary schoolteacher.

My first ever placement was in a primary school in the north of Scotland. I arrived fresh-faced, eager and early on my first day. I remember feeling a heady concoction of terror and excitement. Shaken *and* stirred, I spotted a woman standing at the door, someone I'd describe as a proper scary wee woman. This was the headteacher, my new boss. *Gulp!*

I tried to look confident but, hey, I was 18 and three-quarters. She stopped me and asked, 'Are you our student, son?'

Of course being called 'son' on your first day makes you feel very grown up. 'Yes', I replied through a false smile.

'Male?' she pondered, her observation skills honed to ninja level. 'Right, before you go in, do not forget the first rule of teaching, son.'

I thought, 'This is perfect, I'm not even through the door and am already about to learn something. And not any old rule,

the headteacher's first rule of teaching. Sock it to me scary wee lady.'

The headteacher looked at me very seriously and said, 'Don't smile 'til Christmas!'

I stood for a moment and thought this must be a joke. Surely no one would ever encourage another person – especially one who's new and enthusiastic – *not* to smile for the next four months. I checked her face for any signs of humour. I did a double-check for the lowest form, sarcasm. There were none.

I've subsequently found that 'Don't smile 'til Christmas' is a well-used piece of advice for newbies in education, and not just north of the border. Just as I was trying to get my head around this pearler, she turned and walked away, watting her hand down the corridor. 'Staffroom son, second door on the right.'

Whoosh, I was excited again. The staffroom! I had never been in an actual staffroom before. As a child we were never allowed in the staffroom. I'd stood outside a few and remember walking past as the cigarette smoke poured out from underneath the door, but actually venturing into one? This was new territory. I was about to step into grown-up land.

I stood in front of the second door on the right, the *'salle de professeur'*, as it said on the sign (it was a very cosmopolitan school), and composed myself. Deep breath, and I'm in. It was just how I imagined, a perfect rectangle of chairs, a table in the middle strewn with newsletters and biscuits, pigeon holes crammed full of paper down one side and the kitchen area at the back. I felt like I had made it. I was in. This was the inner sanctum. I was a grown-up.

I sat down and very quickly a woman approached me, 'Excuse me son, you're sitting in Anne's chair'. I remembered them telling me at uni that some staffrooms were a bit funny about this, how certain individuals would always sit in the same seat. I moved, awkwardly, to the adjacent seat.

'Go and get yourself a coffee, son,' someone said.

Awkward again. I have a caffeine allergy you see. But I was straight out of school and still in the mindset of being the pupil, so I did as I was asked and made a coffee. I stood there stirring it, thinking: 'I'm going to die. I haven't even made it into the classroom yet and someone is going to have to phone my mother.'

But I was rescued. Another woman approached me and pointed out, 'Excuse me son, you're using Anne's mug.'

Anne was causing me problems and I hadn't even met her. In fact, I never did. She was always off. With stress. Too many people using her mug, apparently.

So there I stood, Monday morning in the kitchen area of the staffroom in my new place of work, a 45-year career stretched out before me. I didn't know where to sit, what to drink from or who to talk to. I stood for a few more minutes. No one spoke to me.

I cupped my coffee, tempted to take a sip just to take away the numbness. Maybe death wasn't such a bad thing? People were coming and going; some stood in conversation with others. I listened, I watched and my unease started to grow into worry. Forty-five years began to feel like a life sentence. There was a feeling about the room that is best described as grumpiness. There was plenty of chatter, but the undercurrent was most definitely an unease with the world. There was a distinct atmosphere. And believe it or not I began to doubt my entire choice of career. Think about this for a moment, I began to doubt my entire choice of career based entirely on other people's conversations, moods, energy, attitudes, mindsets and faces.

You'll have met these people. You might even be one.

Just as I began to think I had made a huge mistake, it all changed. The entire feeling in the room flipped upside down with the introduction of just one member of the team.

I later learned this woman wasn't in any official leadership role and she wasn't a classroom teacher; she was a classroom assistant – a very important role, but not a very lofty position in the overall pecking order. She just floated into the staffroom like Mary Poppins. Practically perfect in every way. It was like she had rays of light coming out of her face. She just lit the room up and you could feel it. Everyone seemed to smile, the room lifted, conversations changed. People were delighted to see her. In less than five seconds the grumpiness had been exorcised.

Just to clarify – and so the enormity hits you, like it did me – this lady hadn't even said anything, she'd just walked into the room.

I stood there thinking, 'WOW! Who are you? You've not even opened your mouth, I want to be you. I want to be Mary Poppins.' I had never had this thought before! Eighteen years of age and my life's biggest challenge had now become, 'How do I channel my inner Mary Poppins'?

It instantly threw me back to when I was in school as a child and the types of teachers I encountered. In fact, let's get interactive; think about the teachers you had as a child. There will be two types you remember immediately: there are your Mary Poppinses and there are your Mr Bankses.

Let's look at the Mary Poppins type first. These people are pure magic – delightful, hardworking, engaging and fun. They listened, they valued you, they actually taught you and you looked forward to their classes. At times life-changing, always a joy. They made a positive difference in your life and you can remember them to this day.

And now the Mr Banks type. Let's just be blunt. These men and women are a disgrace and shouldn't be allowed in the classroom in the first place. Angry, miserable, bored, negative, unhappy, complain-y people. You learned next to nothing about their subject but you remember the negative impact they had on you to this day.

And then there are all the ones who sit between these two extremes. You won't be able to remember them straight away. There's a good reason for this … *they're not memorable!*

So there I was, stood in the '*salle de professeur*', thinking to myself, 'Who are you going to be Gavin? Mary Poppins or Mr Banks? They both have impact. Huge impact. Life-lasting impact. Just in two polar-opposite ways.'

I made a pact with myself that day. Whatever I do in life, whatever I find myself faced with, I'm Mary Poppins.

All of a sudden the lady with the sunbeams shining out of her face turned, and with a big smile came towards me. 'Are you Gavin?'

'Open different doors, you may find a you there that you never knew was yours. Anything can happen.'

Mary Poppins

The first person to address me by name! 'Yes,' I stuttered, 'and are you Mary?'

(I didn't really ask that ...)

'Yes, that's me,' I beamed back.

'You're with me this morning Gavin. In the nursery. Let's go play!'

And with rays of light coming out of our faces, we floated off down the corridor.

As we approached the nursery – I kid you not – she turned and said, 'And today, Gavin, we're making kites.'

BOOM ... she really was Mary Poppins

There's something about Mary ...

We were tempted to end the chapter in Fatboy Slim style, *right here, right now*, with the sentence above. But Andy can't help chucking his PhD at you, so while Gav goes off to make a kite, here's the science behind his 'Mary Poppins experience'.

I've been studying the science of human flourishing for the last 12 years (in the UK. *Yes, really!*) and have gained insight into information that was locked up inside pay-per-view academic journals. These tomes are written in such dense scientific jargon that only rigorously trained researchers could extract any meaning. So I donned a white coat and infiltrated their world. I became one of them. An interloper.

A translator.

If I told you that you could have 27% more energy and 24% more happiness, you'd be interested, right? If I told you this energy was clean, green and renewable, I'd have your undivided attention. If I threw in the fact that this extra energy/happiness combo is totally free, you'd be like, where do I sign?

I've discovered what you already know: that too many people are counting down to their weekends, next holiday or retirement, accidentally falling into the trap of wishing their lives away.

But there are a few outliers – people who are bursting with energy and enthusiasm. The Marys; folk whose happiness and positivity leak out into the people around them.

Brace yourself for some big thoughts. As we go through life we accumulate experiences and add layers of who we think we should be. As RuPaul says, 'We're born naked, the rest is just drag'. We're striving to be a good parent or a good employee, partner, lover and carer, whilst also keeping on top of our emails. There's a certain etiquette about how we think we should behave in certain situations. And, to be frank, life can get a bit serious. We learn that Mondays are bad and Fridays are good. Like the clay Buddha, we become mummified under layers and layers of who we think we're supposed to be.

But what if all those layers mean we sometimes forget who we really are? And therefore the secret of eternal happiness isn't to learn a whole load of new stuff, but rather to peel back some of the layers to reveal the shine inside. It's more than self-improvement. We call it 'self-remembering'.

But how did we forget in the first place?

The simple truth is that we're social animals. We're wired to copy. Humans have an overwhelming desire to fit in that manifests in conformity of thinking and behaviour. Look around you. Most people are exhausted, harried and worn. Your desire to fit in means you learn to do the same. So here's the rub – you can wait (*and wait, and wait …*) for everyone else to shine and then you can join in.

Chances are you'll die waiting.

Or you can do what the happiness outliers do. Realizing that life is a short and precious gift, they flick a switch in their thinking and go for it. The sublime realization is that a candle can be used to light other candles. And lighting other candles doesn't diminish your light, it creates more.

> '*I like people who shake other people up and make them feel uncomfortable.*'
>
> *Jim Morrison*

For Mary, shining is not a waiting game, it's a starting game.

When was the last time you just stopped and thought about the impact that you have? At work, in your team, on your customers, in your family, amongst your friends, online, on the train …

Everyone's heard of paranoia. We're interested in the opposite, 'pronoia'; the sneaky feeling that people are saying nice things about you behind your back. Wouldn't that be a nice affliction to have? Imagine, there might even be whisperings as people conspire to be on your side. Yes, the bastards are out to help you!

And it's totally possible. If you're like Mary, that is. So who is Mary? She's got the same job, same pressures, same work colleagues, same pay structure and working hours as everyone else in that *salle de professeur*. So how come she has sunbeams radiating out of her face? What's she doing that's different? And, more to the point, why the heck is she the only one doing it?

Gav's Mary Poppins experience happened to take place in a work context, so let's examine that before extrapolating it to the big stage show we call 'life'.

'Long-term strategy: Don't be a jerk.'
Seth Godin

Why not have a go and see if you can prove something to yourself? Think about your last working week, get a pen and map yourself against the 16 emotions. Keep it rough and ready – gauging the strength of feeling and approximate time you experienced each one.

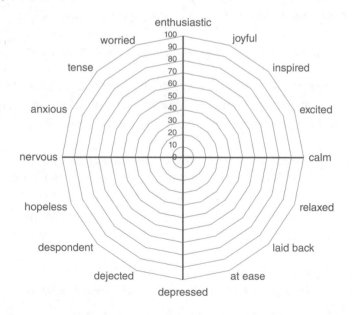

In my research, the top-right quadrant (enthusiastic, joyful, inspired and excited) is summarized as 'engaged'. The bottom-right quadrant (calm, relaxed, laid back and at ease) is 'satisfied'. Bottom left (depressed, dejected, despondent and hopeless) is labelled as 'depression' and top left (nervous, anxious, tense and worried) is labelled as 'anxiety'.

So what?

Well, I graphed a shed load of people onto the diagram and built up a heat map of workplace emotions. The really hot stuff is happening in the top-right quadrant, a space inhabited by what I call '2%ers'. These employees are not only significantly happier, but they also possess bags more energy.

Tying in to the fabulous work of Kim Cameron, positive energy creates feelings of aliveness, arousal, vitality and zest, suggesting, 'It is the life-giving force that allows us to perform, to create and to persist' (p. 49).[1]

Bringing you back to Gav's words, these are the handful of folk who have sunbeams shining out of their faces. The problem with 2%ers? The clue's in the name. There aren't enough of them!

Yet they're crucial. This small minority of people you can think of, right now, are your life-givers. Philosopher Gav nails it non-academically with his Mary Poppins sentence: '*We floated off down the corridor*'. Kim Cameron says the

---

[1] Cameron K. (2013). *Practicing Positive Leadership: Tools & Techniques that Create Extraordinary Results.* Berrett-Koehler.

same thing academically: 'Interacting with positive energizers leaves others feeling lively and motivated … interacting with them builds energy in people and is an inspiring experience' (p. 42).

A point of clarification before we go any further, my 2%ers aren't a bunch of self-nominated Duracell monkeys who bounce in on a dreary Monday all cymbal-clashing and false happy-clappiness. 'Don't those weekends drag? Isn't it great to be back to work?' will, quite frankly, get you slotted into the category of 'some village is missing its resident idiot'.

The 2%ers have been painstakingly sought, filtered through various processes, the most important of which is that they have been nominated by those around them as *someone who makes me feel good*. So, yes, they rate very high on happiness and energy but, crucially, their feel-good factor has leaked. Reminder time: Mary Poppins came into the staffroom and the whole atmosphere lifted.

AND SHE HADN'T EVEN SPOKEN!

Back to the spider diagram, this time with some detail. My research is clear. The conclusion is that 2%ers are satisfied, rating significantly higher than their colleagues on feelings of 'calm', 'laid back', 'relaxed' and 'at ease' – yet they are also experiencing heightened feelings of 'enthusiasm', 'joy', 'inspiration' and 'excitement'; emotions that drive them in their pursuit of something extra. They rate significantly higher in the quadrants of 'satisfaction' AND 'engagement', as well as lower in all aspects of 'depression' and 'stress'. For the purists, 15 of these emotional differences are of statistical significance.

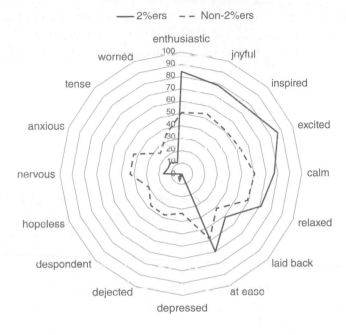

Engagement (the four emotions in the top-right quadrant) is characterized as positive, fulfilling, vigorous and absorbing.[2] In the workplace, engaged employees are more likely to agree with statements such as: 'I eat, live, and breathe my job', 'At my work, I feel bursting with energy', 'I find the work that I do full of meaning and purpose' and 'When I am working, I forget everything else around me.'[3]

Digging deeper into that certain 'something' that Mary had, Kim Cameron's work on vitality examines four types of energy: physical, mental, psychological and relational – only one of which is renewable.

[2] Cameron, 2013.
[3] Schaufeli, Salanova, González-Romá, and Bakker (2002). 'The Measurement of Engagement & Burnout: A Two Sample Confirmatory Factor Analytic Approach.' Journal of Happiness Studies 3, pp. 71–92.

Physical energy is the body's naturally occurring energy, produced by burning calories. Just sitting reading this book will burn calories. Listening to it as an audio book while you're out jogging will burn a whole lot more.

Psychological energy is specifically to do with mental concentration and brain work. In my case, my psychological tank runs low when working on a spreadsheet or attending a long meeting.

Emotional energy is all about experiencing intense feelings and is depleted by, for example, periods of intense excitement or sadness.

But it's the last one that's the biggy. 'Relational energy', in contrast to the other three, is an energy that increases as it is exercised. This form of energy is enhanced and revitalized through positive interpersonal relationships. Cameron describes relational energy as uplifting, invigorating and rejuvenating, and concludes it is 'life-giving rather than life-depleting' (p. 51).[4]

And where does 'relational energy' come from?

People, that's where. The Mary Poppins kind.

The missing book store genre

It boils down to this: is Mary just a weirdo?

The short answer is yes. If we're defining 'weirdo' as someone who deviates from the norm. Mary is a statistical anomaly.

[4] *Cameron, 2013.*

But then, I can't think of any 'normal' people who have changed the world.

So far, we've been talking about work, but we think there's an easy crossover with life. In Baker, Cross and Wooten's[5] study, energizing relationships produced feelings of being 'stimulated', 'up', 'intense' and 'animated'. People explained how energizing relationships made them feel engrossed, enthused and drawn in.

I hope you can see why we're so excited. This goes way above 'satisfaction' with life and into high levels of energy and resilience; way above 'acceptable' into being fully present and happily engrossed. Engagement is associated with drive, vigour and energy.

Basically, 'life satisfaction' sets the bar very low, whereas 'engagement' requires one of Dick Fosbury's bar-raising flops. In short, 2%ers are not ok with 'ok'. You have to *want* to shine, you need to know *how* to shine and you need some resilience in order to stay shining.

It's very easy to lose your lustre, or to use the analogy of a couple of paras ago (minus the prose), there's always some bastard trying to piss on your candle.

If you browse the bookshop shelves you'll find an entire section called 'self-help' and no section called 'help others'. Think of your mission as shining for the right reasons, in the right place, with the right people, and by the right amount in order to help others glow.

Hopefully you are now 'getting' what a 2%er actually is. Maybe you can think of one (sadly, you won't be able to think of many)

---

[5] *Baker, W., Cross, R & Wooten, L. (2003). Positive Organizational Network Analysis & Energizing Relationships in Positive Organizational Scholarship: Foundations of New Discipline, pp 328–342. Cameron, K.S., Dutton, J.E. & Quinn, R.E. (Eds.). San Francisco: Berrett-Koehler.*

and, if the penny has dropped, you will realize that this book is about the modern-day imperative that you need to be one!

In fact, let's rethink that sentence because, of course, you already are a 2%er – *sometimes*. Those times when you feel zestful, full of energy, bouncy, confident, passionate and optimistic. Nobody can feel like that all the time, but everyone can learn to feel amazing more often.

So, cutting to the chase, physical, psychological and emotional energy are depleted during the day. The only way to renew your energy is to mix with other 2%ers.

The chances are you will have experienced both ends of the energy spectrum. At the lower end are the Eeyores or mood hoovers; those with a lifetime of experience on how best to suck every drop of spirit out of you. They're not horrible people, it's much subtler than that. They might be deliberate blockers and naysayers, but most mood hoovers aren't purposefully negative – they've simply learned to be a doom merchant and/or habitual moaner. Their default thinking draws them into an ultra-defensive mindset of spot-the-problem-rather-than-the-solution.

Of course, the mood hoovers might actually be right. Once again, we are not advocating some sort of happy-clappy blue-sky-thinking rainbow-unicorned orgazmatron of positivity. Some ideas and situations are just totally shit. We get that. The weather is sometimes dreadful. People lose their

> 'If you can't pick the people up in your life, for goodness sake don't let them take you down.'
> *Les Brown*

jobs. Relationships break up. Teenagers go off the rails. People die. 'Another work restructure – how thrilling. With fewer jobs to go round. I'm like beyond excited!' is a sure fire way to lose friends and alienate people. Cheshire catting through your grandma's funeral; ditto.[6]

> 'People seem to forget that the core principle of all our differences is as simple as not being an asshole.'
>
> *Anon*

The problem with mood hoovers is that their default negativity kills everyone else's creativity, stone dead. Over time, it's like putting bromide in Tigger's tea. The bounce is extinguished.

The quest

Did you know there are only seven stories? Apparently, all books and films, ever, revolve around one or all of these:

1. Overcoming the monster (Harry Potter).
2. Rags to riches (Cinderella).
3. Quest (Indiana Jones).
4. Voyage and return (Wizard of Oz).
5. Comedy (Hangover 1 & 2).
6. Tragedy (Hangover 3).
7. Rebirth (Grinch).

---

[6] *Unless she's astoundingly wealthy, of course.*

If we're allowed to be so bold, we suggest SHINE attempts them all. By Chapter 3, you're already well into the perilous journey. We've introduced you to mood hoovers but you can expect more monsters. There will be laughs along the way, but also plenty of tears. Essentially, it's a rags to riches story that involves rebirth. Of you. But more than anything, it's a quest, because that's our fave genre.

The quest saga always has the same basic structure, though local details may vary. Each saga begins with a hero receiving a call to adventure which makes him/her abandon their familiar safe environment to venture into the dangerous unknown. Remember, Indiana Jones gave up his job as a lecturer to go after the Arc of the Covenant. Next, our hero undergoes a series of tests and trials, negotiates a few serpents, kills a few baddies, and so on. As a reward s/he wins a magical prize (a golden fleece, a princess, some glass slippers, a chest of treasure, elixir of eternal life, that kind of thing). And, in a final hurrah, the prize is brought back from the kingdom of doom to redeem their community.

Of course, we're not suggesting that we're heroes, swashbuckling away on your behalf. No, no, it's much bigger than that.

We're suggesting YOU are!

Hats off to you. You're already our hero. Maybe it's time to be yours too.

Back in the so-called good old days, local entrepreneurs sold ointments and remedies that would cure anything and everything. Or so they claimed. Snake oil. Fake medicine.

But is there an elixir? A magic cure-all? A universal remedy that would fix psychological and emotional woes? And by fixing them, might there be a knock-on effect physically?

Happiness really will! It's good for your mind, body and soul. It's the ultimate elixir. Forget Indy chasing after the holy grail; happiness is it! Sip from the cup of happiness and everything changes. Your present, but also your past and your future.

So, a big thought to end a big chapter ...

Consciousness involves the experience of knowing and the awareness of the known. Choice emerges from consciousness. If you are not conscious of something, you cannot choose it. Which brings me onto the result of my 120k word door-stop of a thesis. This is by no means a rollercoaster of a thesis crammed with sizzling gypsies, it's a lummox of a thing which, if I were ever to give it an Amazon review, the 1-star would read 'The covers of this book are too far apart'. And that's a review, by me, the author of said door-stop.

Twelve years. One hundred and twenty thousand words. A study of 4000 people. And my principal finding? In one sentence, *what exactly is it about Mary?*

Drum roll ...

Happy/energetic people consciously choose to be positive.

Shush that screaming voice in your head. The one that's shouting: *12 years! For that? How the heck did he string that out to 120k?*

To be fair, it was a struggle. The 'stringing it out' bit. However, the finding isn't quite as obvious as it seems. Remember from a few sentences ago, 'If you are not conscious of something, you cannot choose it'?

Very few people actively choose to carry a positive attitude with them. Yes, that's maybe because the modern world is so full-on and relentless that they get embroiled in busyness to the point that they forget to choose. Or the 'choice' is brow-beaten out of them. But what if it's bigger than that? What if the vast majority of people don't know there's an attitudinal choice available? If you didn't know you could choose, it'd never cross your mind to do so.

Take it from us. You've got lots of attitudinal choices. If getting out of bed in the morning is a chore and you're not smiling on a regular basis, try another choice.

Dirty windows

A young couple moved into a swanky apartment in a new neighbourhood. They sat in their kitchen having breakfast, watching the world go by.

The woman saw her neighbour pegging out the washing. 'That laundry's not very clean,' she tutted. 'She either needs a new washing machine or better washing powder.'

Other than crunching on his toast, her husband remained silent.

His wife's comment was exactly the same the next day. And the next. 'Why on earth is that woman hanging out dirty washing?' She sighed in disgust. 'She needs lessons in basic hygiene!'

And her husband crunched, knowingly.

On the fourth day, his wife plonked herself at the breakfast table with a gleeful smile. 'At last,' she said, pointing at their neighbour's washing line. Her husband followed her gaze to the neatly arranged clothes line where the whites sparkled and the colours shone. 'All of a sudden she seems to have learned to clean properly.'

And her husband broke his silence, 'I got up early this morning and cleaned our windows.'[7]

We're into the realms of some things being so obvious they're hidden in plain sight.

Our eyes are our windows on the world. It's easy to be critical. It's easy for our windows to become grimy.

Fact – not everything in the world is good and bright and fantastic. We're not pretending it is. We're not advocating rose-tinted spectacles, merely that if you clean the shit off your current ones, the world's a lot brighter than you think.

Gav focuses his audiences with this: are you the best *in* your team or are you the best *for* your team? Are you the best *in* the world or best *for* the world?

Remember, no one will remember everything you say, but they will remember exactly how you made them feel. Other books might call it authenticity. Remember our word from earlier: pronoia? What kind of person do you have to be for people to be saying nice things about you behind your back? This

---

[7] Thanks to Kav Vaseer for sharing. Yes, Andy used it in a previous book. He's using it again because it's brilliant.

chapter is about reminding you that you already are that person. *Sometimes!* Our job is to nudge you to live there more often, in which case you will become the kind of person who, without intending it, is a source of marvellous accidents.

It's time to unleash your inner Mary Poppins. That's an interesting thought, but time is short so we'll crack on with the next chapter. We've got kites to fly.

Chapter 4

THAT WEE PIECE OF MAGIC

Previously, in SHINE (you need to read that bit in a US box series voice) *we've covered a whole load of adult material, like sex in the city, small willies, Andy's PhD and shit.*

So it's about time for a kiddie's chapter. Looking through the eyes of a four-year-old we find the world is mud-licious and puddle-jumpingly wondrous. Shockingly, we fail to explain why eyeballs are called eyeballs and fall just short of recommending that you go feral, wearing your leopard skin pants while snaring squirrels in your local park.

Changing gear, we make a point about change via the medium of food (broccoli and sausage rolls, mainly). Then, in a glorious section about play, we introduce you to the X-Box prototype – the 'C-Box' – before regaling a tale of the world's best Tig contest.

Our breathless chapter ends, somewhat epically, by us volunteering to be your Commissioner Gordon, but on one condition – that you'll be our Batman.

Deal?

Excellent!

Let's go play …

'DAAAAD!'

If life had a strapline, it might be something like, 'Stop trying to be perfect and start being remarkable'.

This chapter is a *children's special*. No, not written for children, but it has lashings of children in it. Strictly speaking, it'll be the same child appearing a lot of times, but you get our drift.

The unashamed child-like perspective is to remind you how to have more and more of those miraculous days. It's grounded in pure realism, if you're four, and will act as a shot in the arm, rejuvenating your mojo and equipping you for life as it is. Because, let's face it, that's how life comes at you. The world isn't going to change to accommodate you. If you're waiting for everything to fall into place, for that perfect moment, and then you'll start shining – you'll die waiting. Dimmed into extinction.

The modern world is, on the whole, rather amazing. Yes, we know the news is bad and The Daily Tabloid screams about everything being better back in the day. We're not convinced by that argument. Bring back rickets? Or polio? What about outside toilets? Are those the good old days we're hankering after?

We said the modern world was 'amazing', not 'perfect'.

Contemporary life does provide a significant set of wellbeing challenges, one of the most fundamental being this: humans have an astonishingly versatile, powerful and creative mind/body that thrives in a particular environment – one which allows movement and mobility, one which encourages perspective, horizon and provides natural stimulation. We're built for an environment that promotes creativity and growth.

If you map what we're built for against the world we've created, there's a mismatch. We increasingly live and work in environments that are distinctly hostile to us being the best versions of ourselves. Often we live in a world which is sedentary, artificial, repetitive, screen-based, stressful and lacking in nourishment from community, sunlight, wildness, wisdom and the simplest of wholesome foodstuffs.

Such a divergence manifests in fatigue, obesity and an array of weird and not-so-wonderful degrees of mental ill-health. Just like the Lord, the modern world doth both giveth and taketh away.

The above para distilled into one sentence?

We have a hunter–gatherer mind/body but nothing to hunt or gather.

On the face of it, the solution could be very simple. Jack your job in and spend your days in your leopard skin pants, snaring squirrels in your local park. On balance, that's not such a great idea. We figure you're in the upper quartile of intelligence (you're reading this book for heaven's sake) and you look after yourself pretty well. You go to the gym, eat healthy(ish) food, moisturize and take cod liver oil supplements but, ultimately, those birthday cards still have bigger numbers on them year by year. The days are relentless. But what if it isn't about vitamins and Nivea? What if the secret of eternal youth was in our heads – more specifically our *thinking* – and we could maintain some of that youthful, carefree exuberance that young children manage to generate? They're not fussed about the news. They don't care what day of the week it is because you don't actually learn that Mondays are bad until you start school.

Think back to when you were seven years old and your teacher handed you a reading book that you had read the year before.

How did it make you feel? Well, as an ex-primary
schoolteacher, I'll tell you exactly how it made the children feel
the first time I made this mistake – furious, absolutely furious.

Why? Because at seven years of age we want nothing more than
to be moved up a reading level. We want nothing more than for all
of our classmates to see, hear and hopefully to acknowledge that
we've been moved up a reading level! And of course the only thing
we want more than that is to be able to go home and tell our
parents that we've been moved up a reading level. We're seeking
that look of pride and approval. And if your mum was anything like
mine, she'd wallpaper your new book for you. If you were lucky
you'd get a cool poster of your favourite band. (It's a generation
thing, some of you will have no idea what we're talking about.)

Another thing that always amazed me as a primary schoolteacher
was those moments I was sitting doing my work as all the kids
were doing theirs, and the queue formed to my right-hand side.

Now we've all stood in that queue, we know what it's like. It
usually consists of a row of children with great big smiles on their
faces, saying something along the lines of, 'I'm finished, what's
next?' It's like an absolute need at that age; a want and desire to
learn, to progress, to prove themselves and to embrace the next
challenge. We don't care what others think. We're ready, willing
and more than able to take on the world, to be the best we can
be, to dream and to think big. I often think we should put seven-
year-olds in charge of the Palestine–Israeli spat; it'd be sorted in
less than an hour.

Every single day as a primary schoolteacher my mind was
completely and utterly blown by the attitude those kids showed
towards their daily learning adventure.

But there's a problem with being that age and there's a problem with being at primary school, and it's this: we stop being that age. There's a technical term for it: 'growing up'.

> 'The very things that hold you down are going to lift you up.'
>
> Timothy Mouse, 'Dumbo'

I believe that in growing up too many of us lose something special. Very special. Some hold on to it forever, for others it comes and goes, but for many, it just disappears entirely. I'm going to refer to it as '*that wee piece of magic*'. It's a natural thing that we're all born with. I see it in my own two kids every day.

So what do I actually mean by 'that wee piece of magic'? Let me try and explain …

About three months before my son's fifth birthday we woke at 4am to the sound of him screaming, '*DAAAAD*' as loud as he possibly could. I got the fright of my life and leapt out of my bed. In fact, I didn't even touch the bed, I just landed on two feet and ran for the door (because that's how ninjas respond). As I headed for the door, Kian came running into the room still shouting, '*DAAAAD!*'

Obviously concerned, I stopped him and asked 'What on earth is it Kian? It's four in the morning. What's the matter?'

Perfectly calm, Kian smiled and simply answered, 'I know why they're called eyeballs.'

This, for me, was a moment of magic. Let me explain why.

The fact that it was 4am is irrelevant when the star of the story is only four. Kian had woken up and had a moment of learning, which is cool but it's not the moment of magic. The moment of magic came next.

He shared it.

That's it. It's that simple.

He fucking shared it.

Because that's what you do when you're four, you share stuff. Doesn't matter what you experience or what you discover, you share it. Doesn't matter how big it is or how small it is, you share it. Doesn't matter how exciting it is or how boring it is, how colourful or dull, you share it, because you're four.

But at nearly five, you don't just share it.

You share it from here (*points to chest*), with heart and soul. With passion, energy, excitement and it's always wrapped up in a big ball of wonder. It's beautiful. It's magic.

So why is this relevant to you – a grown up – reading this? How many times in your life have you been asked at work to share best practice, share your knowledge, your inspirations and your ideas? And how often do you actually share, from here (*points to chest*), with heart and soul? With passion, energy and excitement all wrapped up in a big ball of wonder?

There's how we lead. There's how we create a movement. There's how we inspire. There's how we make a difference.

There's how we change the world.

And in case you're wondering, Kian never actually told me why they're called eyeballs. To be fair, that wasn't the point.

Five a day

Kian again.

We were having dinner one night. In fact, we do that most nights. There was broccoli on the plate. Now I don't like broccoli, but my kids love it. They're weird, right? I had broccoli on my plate because that's a good parenting example.

My son leant over, picked up a piece of broccoli from my plate and said, 'Dad, you should eat your greens,' to which I replied, 'And you should stop touching my food.'

'Broccoli is great fun Dad.' I had never heard this sentence before. He continued, 'It can beee stuff'.

Now, instantly my brain showed me lots of pictures of trees We all know broccoli looks like trees. It turned out I was on the right lines, but as he was only four he was streets ahead of me. Holding up the piece of broccoli he said, 'See this piece here Dad, I want you to imagine it's summer time, in fact, no Dad' – he bit the head off the broccoli – 'it's autumn.'

Genius. I sat there thinking isn't it incredible how, at such a young age, we can take anything we want and transform it into anything we want?

Anything.

Of course, at such a young age we find this process much more natural. Firstly, as kids we want things to be better, to be more fun, more exciting. Secondly, we believe it to be possible. And lastly, we know it will be worth the effort.

> 'I always thought that there was at least one person in the stands who had never seen me play, and I didn't want to let him down.'
>
> *Joe DiMaggio (American baseball legend)*

Now think about this from an adult's perspective.

Most adults want things to be better, to always be improving. Most want change. Step one is always the easy part. Step two is where we lose some people. They didn't believe it to be possible. As adults we overthink things to such an extent we convince ourselves we can't do it.

And then there's step three, the Bridget Jones' passion-killer knickers of doom – as adults we know what it means to be told, 'The effort will be worth it in the long run'. It's shorthand for, 'It's going to be awful. It's going to be stressful, messy and we're all going to be exhausted.'

We're reminded of a beautiful quote by Cynthia Occelli: 'For a seed to achieve its greatest expression, it must come completely undone. The shell cracks, its insides come out and everything changes. To someone who doesn't understand growth, it would look like complete destruction.'

At four years of age we don't see destruction. We see adventure and excitement, we just think, 'Bring it on'.

As adults, many of us see hard work, frustration and effort.

It's time more of us rediscovered our inner child.

Just press 'play'

Kian, again. *Again!*

I was sat watching Nick Jr with my kids when I had a lightning bolt of learning from one of the great philosophers of our time, Grampy Rabbit. As Grampy Rabbit was showing all the boys and girls around his Dinosaur Park, his good friend Peppa Pig – herself a great thinker – famously asked Grampy, 'Is it real?'

To which the sagest of all rabbits in the history of bunny civilization replied, 'It's better than real, it's pretend.'

Think back to when you were five years old and someone handed you a cardboard box. What's the first thing you did with it?

Exactly! You got in it. You flew it, drove it, sailed it, transformed it, defended it, ate it. It could be anything. Forget the Xbox. A *cardboard*-box was the ultimate plaything.

The question therefore arises, when was the last time you played in a cardboard box? It might have been last night for all we know, but that's unlikely.

When was the last time you looked at a cardboard box and then looked at a staircase whilst pulling your 'up to no good' face, took the box to the top of the stairs, wedged your adult arse in and slid/tumbled from top to bottom while shouting the word '*WEEEEE*' as loud as you could?

Exactly!

Do it, do it now and then jump onto Twitter and tweet us with the hashtags #CBox and #SHINE.

Now, we're not suggesting for a second that in order for you to be happier, more energetic, more motivated or more successful you have to bobsleigh down your stairs in a cardboard box. However, we want to challenge the way you think about, well, everything really.

When did the day come when some decided that now was the day to stop playing? To stop approaching everyday situations with playfulness, creativity and joy. With intrigue and fun. Did someone tell us it was wrong? Childish? What's childish about play?

Before anyone says, 'Hang on, play is surely only essential for kids', let's just be clear, play doesn't end with childhood.

You can have a happy childhood at any age.

We've all heard the well-known scientific fact that children learn best through play, but have you ever heard this one …

ADULTS LEARN BEST THROUGH PLAY!

Some just need to turn off their TV and become interesting. Or simply just be interested.

Play brings joy. And it's vital for problem solving, creativity and relationships.

Stuart Brown, MD sums it up beautifully in his bestselling book *Play*, where he writes:

'Consider what the world would be like without play. It's not just an absence of games or sports. Life without play is a life without books, without movies, art, music, jokes, dramatic stories. Imagine a world without flirting, no day-dreaming, no comedy, no irony. Such a world would be a pretty grim place to live. In a broad sense, play is what lifts people out of the mundane.'

In his book, Brown compares play to oxygen: 'It's all around us, yet goes mostly unnoticed or appreciated until it is missing'.

Fancy dress top tip:

Andy once went to a fancy-dress party dressed in an oversized suit. He was Tom Hanks from 'Big'.

We need oxygen to breathe. Or we die.

Would it be crazy to think we need play in order to live? Or that without it – in certain ways – we die?

Think about it, play shapes the brain, opens the imagination and invigorates the soul. If we really wanted to stick our necks out, we might even say play can save lives. It certainly enhances them.

It's important to note at this point that the opposite of play is not work. We often hear from delegates at conferences that their workplace and/or boss is *all work and no play*. The two shouldn't have to be separated, we believe they can be, should be and *are* inextricably linked together. What work and play share is creativity.

Many grown-ups tell us they're not very creative. Absolute nonsense, creativity is a function of the human brain, you cannot

not be creative. The problem lies in the fact that many adults and workplaces don't actively practise their creativity. It gets stifled and hidden behind a big list of rules and procedures.

> '1 want to meet the man who saw a turtle and said, people will love the ninja version of that.'
>
> *Anon*

Think about it. Most things that are important to you, excite you, are of interest to you and all things that stir your emotions are the results of creativity. If we were to be more actively creative, losing ourselves in activities that bring us fulfillment, we would feel more alive in the world.

When was the last time you had a game of Tig? You might have a different name for it: Tag, It, Tip, Tuggy or even Dobby!

We dare you to walk up to a colleague tomorrow, tap them on the arm (appropriately, of course), say, '*You're it*' – and run.

Chase games have been around for centuries. Someone 'tigs' you and it's nearly impossible not to immediately then 'tig' someone else. You instantly pick a target, a goal even, create a plan and you're off!

> 'Goals transform a random walk into a chase.'
>
> *Mihalyi Csikszentmihalyi*

Some will chase harder in a game of tig than they will in their own career.

One of the greatest 'Tig' related stories we've ever heard featured in the *Guardian* newspaper. The following story is told by Joe Tombari …

As teenagers, a group of friends and I spent every spare moment at school playing tig. The game developed into more than just chasing each other round the playground; it involved strategy and cunning. But when I failed to tig someone in the last moments before school broke up for summer – he'd locked himself in his car to avoid it – I resigned myself to forever being "it".

We all went our separate ways, off to college or moving away for work, so the game fizzled out. Then a reunion brought the 10 of us together again a few years later and someone suggested reviving it. Since we had busy lives and lived hundreds of miles apart, we agreed on three rules. First, we would play it only in February each year; second, you were not allowed immediately to tig back the person who had tigged you; and finally, you had to declare to the group that you were "it".

Now we are grown men, we don't run like Usain Bolt, so subterfuge and collusion have become our weapons. Eleven months of the year are spent planning. Collaborating with a friend is where the fun is – we can spend hours discussing approaches.

I was tigged spectacularly a few years back when a friend popped round to show me his new car. As I approached it, Sean sprang out of the boot where he'd been hiding and tigged me. He'd flown 800 miles from

Seattle to San Francisco just to stop being "it" – to shrug off the "mantle of shame", as we call it.

Some things we did early on we wouldn't do now – like when Mike sneaked into Brian's house at night, crept into the bedroom and woke him up to tig him, surprising the life out of him and his girlfriend.

Perhaps one of the most unexpected tigs was during Mike's father's funeral. During the service, he felt a hand on his shoulder and turned to find Joe mouthing, "You're it." Afterwards, he said his father would have approved, because he found our game hilarious.

When February arrives, you feel as edgy as a deer in hunting season, locking doors and checking under cars to avoid being caught. When a friend stops answering his phone, you know he's up to something – and your days are numbered. Patrick, who does everything he can to avoid being caught, sometimes spends February in Hawaii. When he learned that he was likely to be tigged as he arrived at the airport, he hired a man to hold up a card with his name on it in arrivals, so one of us would wait near it. Then he slipped out of another exit.

As well as nerve-racking, it's hugely enjoyable and I love the ingenuity involved. When the game had a lull a few years back, my daughter persuaded me to reactivate it; we disguised ourselves as an elderly couple and surprised Joe in a restaurant. His double take was classic.

Sometimes the strategies don't come to fruition. Mike once flew to Boston and staked out Chris's place, hiding

in bushes and searching in bars, only to discover after
two days that he was away for the weekend.

The best thing about the game is that it has kept us
in touch over all these years – it forces us to meet
and has formed a strong bond between us, almost like
brothers. How many forty-somethings can say they
still see nine friends they went to school with? We joke
that we'll still be playing in our retirement homes. I plan
to use a wheelchair instead of a Zimmer frame, because
it's faster.'

Stop pretending to be normal

Play quite simply brings us to life. You could say that play is
seriously fun. Remember, it saves lives, right?

Let's try and break down the concept of play in the context of
actually being an adult. There's a plethora of science out there
around play and it teaches us about many valuable benefits, such
as the development of physical, emotional, social and cognitive
skills as well as self-confidence, self-esteem, experimenting with
emotions, resilience, social intelligence, group interaction and
problem solving.

All great stuff, but what actually goes into it? Does it really fit in
our sensible grown-up world, our workplace?

Here's our take on it.

Play can be great fun, but not always. Play involves a process of
imagination, creativity and innovation. Individually these beauties

stand strong, each one a superpower in its own right. Collectively they change the world. Your world.

You might say imagination is the easy part. The thinking part. But thinking can easily become over-thinking, something many of us grown-ups do incredibly well. Rumination is over-thinking. Like cows chewing the cud, we chew over our problems, several times.

This is where creativity comes into its own; it allows us to do something meaningful with our imagination. Imagination is about seeing the impossible or unreal. Creativity is using imagination to unleash the potential of existing ideas in order to create new and valuable ones.

Where imagination can tell a remarkable story, creativity can make imagination possible. Innovation uses imagination and the power of creativity to measurably improve on what exists today.

Let's just repeat that…

Innovation uses imagination and the power of creativity to measurably improve on what exists today.

It sounds like something from a superhero movie, except in this instance we all have the ability to do this. We all have these superpowers to improve on what exists today. Yes, we're all real life superheroes with real life superpowers.

'I'm normally not a praying man, but if you're up there, please save me Superman.'

Homer Simpson

Which brings us full circle. Many argue Batman isn't really a superhero as he doesn't actually have any superpowers. He's just a rich guy with a butler. But his ability to imagine, create and innovate is truly remarkable and second to none.

Commissioner Gordon once said to Batman, 'You're going to make a difference. A lot of times it won't be huge, it won't be visible even. But it will matter just the same.'

We'll be your Commissioner Gordon if you promise to be our Batman. Stop pretending to be normal. *'You're going to make a difference. A lot of times it won't be huge, it won't be visible even. But it will matter just the same.'*

Pants on the outside might be a step too far. But, hey, that duvet cover would make a really cool cape.

Hell yeah.

TRIPLETS WILL ALMOST CERTAINLY CHANGE YOUR LIFE

Chapter 5 is our Spartacus – an overblown, over budget, sweeping Technicolor epic. Starting with an all-inclusive life, we then go Trogg-like, introducing you to the wild thing that makes your heart sing.

But it's a bucking bronco of a wild thing. If you're going to get aboard, it'll need taming, hence our three things that will enable you to saddle up: HUGGs, botheredness and strengths, introduced like you've never heard before.

There's more beside. The abandoned wellie field of dreams is worth a mention, as is our advice to live a one-buttock life.

I'm Spartacus. No, *I'm* Spartacus.

Ready for the ride of your life?

Good.

Saddle up. Hold tight. *We're away* …

A groundhog life

Gav was sitting at breakfast on day 14 of his five-star all-inclusive family holiday and twice heard the word, 'samey'.

All-inclusive is great. It's there for the taking; literally, everything. You can have your pick of the starters, all the salads, mains, desserts, any drink you can imagine. Even ice-cream. In fact, you can have it all. Twice if you want.

You take and take and take.

It's great to begin with, but soon it doesn't matter what you choose, it becomes repetitive. Bland even. You feel fat, slow and bloated. You end up paying extra to escape. You eat out, something other than groundhog burgers. The dream became 'samey'.

They have a word for everything in boffin-land. For 'samey' read 'habituation' or the over-complicated 'hedonic treadmill'. Whatever you do in life eventually becomes 'normal', and therefore even the most exhilarating activities, after a while, can become a bit humdrum.

It's not just all-inclusive holidays. A pay rise, cocaine, rollercoaster rides, your new car, your job, your partner, sex … even life itself. All these things are magnificent at first but then you kind of get used to them.

Worst top tip ever:

Plan to be spontaneous, tomorrow.

So you need to crank things up, move, fidget, try something new, give up something that's not working, buy some new knickers, learn to play the piano, change your thinking, read a book, go to St Petersburg.

But never settle for samey.

Wild thing, you make my heart sing

The Troggs knew it as far back as 1966. Not only did their 'wild thing' make their heart sing, it also made them feel groovy before finally admitting that 'wild thing, I think I love you.'

We do too.

Gav recently rediscovered Maurice Sendak's book, *Where the Wild Things Are*, an absolute favourite from his childhood. There's so much to drool over, particularly his sentiment that, 'There must be more to life than having everything'. I mean, for a start, where would you put it all?

With the most incredible artwork, I can vividly remember the adventures my older brother and I undertook in the hope we would discover – quite literally – where the wild things were.

One of the most popular children's books of all time, this multi award-winning tale seems to tell a very different story when you go back and revisit it as an adult. Thirty years on the artwork's still awesome, but I am massively surprised to discover the entire story is a mere ten sentences long: 338 words to be exact, *but* 338 words that now exude very different themes.

It's no longer just weird monsters in a weird world. Now, its themes of loneliness, growth and dreams, all of which I definitely missed the first time around when I was six, are totally relatable to a 30-something. Could it be that I now connect more with this book in my adult years than I ever did as a child? Do we, as adults, now know what it really means to be lonely, to chase a dream and crave something new, some 'thing', some *wild thing?*

It's funny, I can't ever remember a time in my life when I *wasn't* hoping to find where the 'wild things' are. Of course, we all have different 'wild things' that we dream about or are in search of. 'Things' that excite us, scare us, shake us, make us and awaken us.

I recently learned that *Where the Wild Things Are* was originally titled *Where the Wild Horses Are*, and was intended, of course, to feature fillies, foals and mares. I hate horses, they're way more scary than 'wild things'. I think it's their big faces. Editor Ursula Nordstrom adored the original title, finding it poetic and beautiful, but there was one problem – Sendak couldn't draw horses. When he told his editor that the whole horse thing wasn't going to work out, he recalls her 'acid tone[d]' response: 'Maurice, what *can* you draw?'

'*Things*', he said, and so 'things' he drew. For the uninitiated, think Trolls. Or perhaps the Gruffalo.

Andy and I make a living out of talking to people. Often it's a big crowd at a conference, but sometimes it's a smaller gathering of the clans, more up-close and personal where you can see the whites of their eyes. Every day, after every gig, we both have wonderful conversations with people from the audience. So often they tell us that we have given them a renewed belief that they can walk out of the room and fulfil all sorts of crazy 'things'. They often speak of the desire to grow and achieve their dreams. Every day we hear, 'There're so many things I want to go do'. And of course, when we ask what those things are, the reply we hear so often is 'just things'. Most people can't articulate what their 'things' are but they're there, lurking at the back of your potential.

> **For sale**: Used tombstone, perfect for someone named Homer HendelBergenHolnzel. One only.

Here lies the problem: we allow the very 'things' we don't really want to get in the way of the very 'things' we really do want. Especially when we don't define the 'things'.

So our advice is simple: just go do the things. Write them down and go do them. Stop wishing. Quit hoping. Cease kicking your 'things' into the long grass. Bring them from the back of your potential into the foreground In touching distance. Be done with messing.

Do what Maurice did. Draw them, bring them to life so you know what it is you're striving towards (unless your 'things' involve horses ... they're really hard to draw, apparently).

The plain truth is that most people coast through life without ever bothering to work out what their 'things' actually are. Especially the wild ones. Until, of course, it's too late and you're on that all-too-familiar death bed of *coulda, woulda, shouda*. What a sad way to go, never even giving your wild things a run for their money.

A few folks have specific and measurable 'things', not many have written these 'things' down. Fewer still have 'wild things'. Next to nobody has ever drawn their 'things' and one in a million has got excited enough to create a specific plan to make these 'things' a reality.

We'd like to take a few pages to address that.

Many years ago, Maurice Sendak was asked if he could share some of his favourite comments from readers that he'd got over the years. Apparently, he once received a charming letter from a young boy named Jim. In return, Sendak drew a 'wild thing' and posted it off as a thank you.

A few days later, the artist received another letter, this time from the little boy's mum: 'Jim loved your card so much he ate it.'

Sendak recalls that as one of the highest compliments he ever received. The lad didn't care that he'd received an original Maurice Sendak drawing. He saw it, loved it and ate it.

We want you to love your wild things so fucking much that someone wants to eat them.

But how do we ever discover where the wild things really are? And does drawing or writing down your 'things' really make them delicious, or is it just a myth?

Andy has a thing about 'things', which we'll come to in a mo. Meantime, we're offering you a blank page to draw your 'thing(s)'. The wilder the better. Think of this as the first stage of taming your wild bucking bronco of a dream.

Trust us. We're going somewhere with this. Get your crayons and draw what you want in life. Just one rule, you MUST get excited! Work out specifically what your wild things are and get arty. Draw them. Create them. Protect them. Cherish them. Be them. Work hard for them. Earn them. Eat them!

Most of all, colour them in (we dare you to colour in like Mr Messy, outside of the lines).

My wild things...

Please take a picture of your wild thing(s) and tag it with #WildThing #Shine.

As Maurice once wrote: 'There should be a place where only the things you want to happen, happen.' It's time to create that place and let the wild rumpus start.

It might just pull you off the ground and let your inner child run wild.

Andy, your turn …

The abandoned welly field of dreams

Gav's gone for a lie down.

For me, goal setting is the biggest personal development quagmire of them all. Kevin Costner had his field of dreams ('build it and they will come') which works really well in movie-land. But in the real world the field of dreams is the tar pit of self-help where most wellies get stuck. Cast your eye afar and it's wellies all the way, abandoned by their owners who have given up.

> 'Your future hasn't been written yet. No one's has. Your future is whatever you make it. So make it a good one.'
>
> *Doc Brown, 'Back to the Future'*

Often, the bog is one of complexity. I remember reading a book where the prescribed goal-setting process was the equivalent of your A-level revision timetable, a thing of such intricate beauty and elaborate planning that you had no time to actually revise.

You've probably seen those adverts for crazily expensive watches that are big and bold enough to scream, 'Look at me,

I've made it. My watch costs the equivalent of your annual salary. Schmuck.'

These watches are built so that if you get run over by a tank, you will be flattened but your timepiece can indeed be passed down to your next of kin. There's one I'm looking at, right now, on the internet. It's water resistant to 2000 metres.

Hold it right there. *It'll tell the time at depths of two kilometres?*

I once dived into a three-metre pool in Majorca, sank to the bottom and felt my head implode. Apparently, at about 30 metres nitrogen bubbles start to develop in your blood, and my lazy Google search suggests the freediving world record is held by Herbert Nitsch. He managed 214 metres, just about killing himself in the process. Good news for Herbert: even if he had been crushed by the pressure, his watch would have survived.

Credit where it's due – well done, watchmakers. You've over-engineered something to the point of pointlessness. A depth of five metres would be ample for me. You could do a special one for Herbert that was good for, say, 250 metres?

But you've gone to the trouble of designing kit that can survive something that will never be achieved. We can't help thinking that's a lot of money and time wasted on a surplus 1.8 kilometres.[1]

Look here, folks, it's not just watchmakers. Sometimes we over-engineer goals too. So far, all we've done is ask you to draw a

---

[1] *My re-work of Stu Spendlow's original idea. Thanks mate.*

picture. Your wild thing needs taming. Once aboard you need two more passengers.

Saddle up …

Botheredness

Let's be blunt, most people live well within their limits. There seems little point in being energized below your maximum and behaving below your optimum. It's like wearing a 2 km watch in the bath or driving a Lamborghini at 27 mph. Or worse, it's like being in possession of a whole load of superpowers that you fail to use. I mean, who would you rather be, Wonder Woman or Diana? Superman or Clark Kent?

You may not even know you have superpowers. They can be heavily disguised: musical, sporting, academic, dance, art, bricklaying, history, numbers, writing, cooking, kindness, positivity, making people laugh, listening, public speaking, coding, acting, organizing, science, teaching, leading, caring, fixing, inventing, figuring things out, technology, imagineering … any of these abilities will enable you to make money. But only if you discover them and bring them to life.

Delving (yet again) into deep stuff that most books don't tell you, at the core of all human behaviour, most people's needs are more or less similar. We want more positive experiences because they make us feel good and they're easy to handle. It's negative experience that we all struggle with. Therefore, what we get out of life is not determined purely by the good feelings we desire but by what bad feelings we're willing and able to sustain to get us to those good feelings.

For example, if you want to lose a bit of weight, you know that you will have to burn off more calories than you consume. That's pretty much the only way it works. So, yes, you want to lose weight but not if you have to stop eating cake. Or go to the gym. Or, heaven forbid, both! So, you wanting to achieve your goal means less than your desire for an easy life. Similarly, you want to start up your own business but that means risk, uncertainty and long hours.

So, counter-intuitively, the question may be less about what you want to achieve and more like, '*What pain are you willing to sustain to achieve it*'? Paradoxically, what if the quality of your life is not determined by the quality of your positive experiences, but your willingness to tolerate negative experiences?

Think about it. Could it be that the barriers in life are put there to show how badly you want something? Or, the same meaning but worked the other way around, if the challenge we face doesn't scare us, then it's probably not that important.

That, dear reader, is a remarkably big thought. So, in the interests of challenging you, it's worth pondering what your three big goals might be, and what you're willing to give up to achieve them.

Activity: What am I willing to sacrifice?

We're asking you for three achievements, one at work, one family and one random exciting goal:

#1 big thing I want to achieve at work

What I'm willing to *give up* to achieve it

#1 big thing I want to achieve in family time

What I'm willing to *give up* to achieve it

#1 other big thing that I want to achieve

What I'm willing to *give up* to achieve it

> **In it to win it**
>
> Interviewer to Jamie Vardy: 'You've got a 5000-1 chance of winning the league.'
>
> Vardy: 'So we've got a chance.'
>
> (Jamie Vardy: Stocksbridge Park Steels footballer who somehow ended up winning the Premier League with a 5000-1 shot, Leicester City.)

So, ear plugs at the ready, we're going to get a little shouty. *GET BOTHERED!*

Hywel Roberts has invented the word 'botheredness' for this very occasion. We hand-on-heartedly cannot think of anything you will do that is more important than raising your levels of botheredness above the national average of 5.2.

Yes, it takes effort. But, my goodness, it's worth every ounce.

Not so SMART

Stretching yourself is good. But to maintain your motivation you need to know where you're stretching to. You need a goal, but heaven forbid, not a SMART one. We're begging you. We're not even going to trot out the acronym behind SMART lest we nod off before we've finished typing.

Raise your sights. In modern terminology, we encourage you to 'go large'. You've drawn your wild thing, a mouth-wateringly exciting 'thing' to aim for, so the next question is how?

It's properly massive. *Where do I start?*

Rewind. A few years ago, I went on a training course run by a heroic genius called David Hyner and he introduced me to

Huge Unbelievably Great Goals (HUGGs). So I got home and did one. At that time I had an idea swirling in my head about a children's book based on my pet dog. What if, while I was at work and my kids were at school, my mutt went around town catching baddies and solving crimes? What if she was a secret agent, a bit like James Bond but a dog, undercover as an ordinary family pet. What if she was a Spy Dog?

> 'Whatever you can do, or dream you can, begin it. Boldness has genius, power, and magic in it.'
>
> *W.H. Murray*

Bragging alert, but 22 titles and half a million book sales later, I'm telling you, this HUGG thing really works. I've even branched out into 'Spy Cat'! I'm wondering, Is 'Spy Ferret' too far?

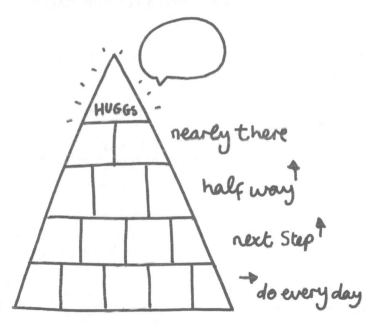

nearly there

half way ↑

next step ↑

→ do every day

Here's how it works. The trick is to write your *huge unbelievable great goal* in the bubble at the top of the pyramid, and to make it compelling. That means not only is it a wild 'wild thing', but also that you really have to want it. It has to excite you. Whatever you drew needs summarizing in one explosive sentence in the bubble at the top of the pyramid.

And when you've written it, stop and have a think. Chances are, you can write it better.

So, for example, '*To set up as a life coach*' is fine, but '*To be the best life coach in the UK*' is finer.

'*To get promoted at work*' is nice. '*To become the best leader for my organization*' is nicer.

'*To be a good mum*' is all well and good, but '*To be the best mum in the world*' is weller and gooder.

'*To get fit*' is stretching, whereas '*to enter and run two half marathons this year*' is stretchier.

'*To lose some weight*' is laudable. '*To look amazing naked*' is less lardable.

Get the HUGG (aka 'wild thing') phrased correctly and work backwards from your inspiring vision.

Start at the bottom of the pyramid and look up. What things do you have to start doing, TODAY AND EVERYDAY, that will move you towards your wild thing? When the bottom rung is filled in, you go to the next level of the pyramid. When you've started doing the things on the bottom row, what next? And next? *And after that?*

When you're finished, you will have a proper HUGG, your wild bucking bronco of a thing, all tamed and rideable. Stick it on your bedroom wall. It will tell you what the huge goal is, and give you a simple set of things to do, or habits to adopt, that will move you forward.

There are a few more pieces to slot in, but your wild thing should start looking less wild. All those things in the boxes are doable, right? But they take a bit of effort. Which is why we introduced botheredness. Life is a never-ending upward spiral. If you think you're ever allowed to stop climbing, I'm afraid you've missed the point. The joy is in the climb itself. Plain simple English yet again, that means a rethink of your thinking so that when there's a challenge, you move away from rolling your eyes and huffing that, 'It's not fair' to a steely-eyed nod of, 'Bring it on'.

There are no guarantees. You will need some luck along the way. In fact, let's change the guarantees sentence: there is only *one* guarantee – your 'wild thing' won't happen by accident.

It will only happen if you take sustained action.

Your inner superhero

But, with goal-setting, there's more. There's the conjoined triplets of 'wild thing', 'botheredness' and one more …

Back to our earlier point. We meet a lot of 'Dianas' and 'Clarks', but not many Wonder Women or Super Men. It's your responsibility to tap into your inner superhero and, if you do, it might have the fortunate side effect of bringing out the powers in those around you.

At a 'celebrity' level, *Time* magazine's 'Person of the 20th Century' would have been consigned to the dustbin of history if we'd focused on his failings. When our celeb was growing up he was referred to as the 'dopey one' and he struggled with words to the point that his family feared he'd never learn to speak. He struggled at school, with one teacher telling him he'd never amount to anything and was wasting everyone's time. He muddled through college with uneven grades and struggled to find a job. Our man wanted to be a teacher, but it took him nine full years to land his first teaching job. As if all these weaknesses weren't enough, he was unbelievably absent-minded. Famously, he couldn't remember his own phone number.

This is hardly the stuff of comic books – but of course all we've talked about are his weaknesses. Fortunately, he didn't focus on his weaknesses, but his strengths. Our hero's strength lay in creative thinking – imagining thought experiments that involved theoretical physics. Rather than thinking in words, he thought in pictures. He imagined what things would look like if he were to travel on a bullet at the speed of light and whether space might curve, so the distance between two points is not necessarily a straight line.

With his incredible imagination, he helped to prove the existence of atoms and dreamt up science's most famous equation: $E = MC^2$. With his brilliant thoughts, he revolutionized science.

So, guess what, Einstein was like you and I – genius at some things and spectacularly bad at others. Fortunately, he worked hard to develop his strengths and didn't let his weaknesses hold him back.

And that's what made him stand head and shoulders above so many others. Remember, we're talking about achieving wild things, huge unbelievably great goals that sit on the edges of your achievability. You will never get there by plodding along. Hence, the conjoined triplet of 'wild things' and 'botheredness' is 'strengths'; finding and playing to them, that is.

Sadly, our preoccupation with fixing weaknesses also does a great hatchet job of diminishing the strengths on the other side. It creates a whole load of averageness and means nobody will be outstanding at anything. Eradicating weaknesses creates middling, run-of-the-mill, Jacks-of-all-trades.

Activity: Unleashing your inner strengths

What are you good at?

What are you great at?

What are the things that you find effortless?

What (and/or who) gives you energy?

Reflecting on the questions above, what are your strengths? (If you can't think of any, change the question to 'If I asked your best friend, what would they say your strengths are?')

What do they look like in action?

Give an example of when you used them.

How can you use them more?

What would happen if you did?

Mojo

There's an awful lot written about motivation and, yes, a lot of it is *awful* – over-complicated 'self-actualization', 'operant', 'cognitive dissonance', 'expectancy/instrumentality/valence', 'efficacy' twaddle. It's 50 shades of unnecessary pain. If you want to be tied up and beaten before we reveal the glorious truth, that's fine, but you'll have to self-flagellate.

We don't deal in pain.

Let's give you an example of what happens when it all comes together. Andy was recently doing some work with a senior leadership team in a school. Despite working themselves to near exhaustion, the school's results were muddling through on 39% A to C grades, the benchmark being 50. The head was troubled by their inability to get out of 'special measures', a suffocating category created by the school inspectorate to indicate a severe arse-kicking. Ironically, in school report terms, it is very much 'could do much better'.

'Special measures' means the pressure is really on, and this school had battened down the hatches and was squeezing extra work out of everyone and monitoring performance so you couldn't go for a shit without filling in a form. That might be an exaggeration, but I promise you this bit is true: the head had cancelled Christmas on the grounds that, 'It's not a priority like Maths or English; but good news,' she croaked as I peered into her bloodshot eyes, 'it looks like it's all been worthwhile because results have improved from 39 to 41.8%.'

Her smile was weak and mine non-existent. She'd fallen into the age-old trap of doing the same, but harder.

'So what's the best school in this city achieving?' I asked.

'Oh, well they have a different catchment,' she began. 'They have supportive parents...'

'... And what are they achieving?' (I deliberately butted in to head off her excuses at the pass.)

'84%,' she said. 'But ...'

'So what are you going to do to beat them?'

Because, you see, I genuinely think that's an exciting question. It's not coming at the future from the past, it's looking at the future through a different lens – the lens of 'How awesome do we want to be?' rather than, 'How rubbish are we right now?'

Cutting to the chase, a wild thing, a huge dollop of botheredness and some strengths-finding has led that school out of the quagmire. And the best bit? Christmas is back on!

While the goose is fattening, we'd like to turn to Ben Zander for our final thought in this epic trawl through the tar-pit of goal-setting. If this is really to be THE chapter, there's a wonderful analogy there for the taking.

Zander talks about the transformation that happens when a young person learns to love music. For a while (sometimes years) they trudge along. For most, the early days are a chore. Most parents will have suffered Three Blind Mice on a recorder, or caterwauling scales on the violin. In classic Eric Morecambe language, they're hitting all the right notes but not necessarily in the right order. And, in these difficult early stages, they often quit and your ears can stop bleeding.

Except a few. The ones who have stickability and passion. The few who care. These kids lean forward and begin to play. They engage, either with the teacher or with the music. They achieve some early breakthroughs, maybe playing a piece that they recognize. As they connect, they lift themselves off the piano seat, suddenly becoming what Zander calls *'one-buttock players'*. They're lifted by passion and engagement. And, from here on in, they experience giant leaps of learning.

If we're allowed to stretch Zander's wonderful analogy beyond music, we encourage you to stick at life until something clicks. 'Wild things', 'botheredness' and 'strengths'; the triplets that will thrust you centre stage.

We want you to lean forward and start living. Life should thrill you – lift you off your seat. There should be less caterwauling and more 'Four Seasons'.

Be one of the few. Yes, in a sentence that's never been written in the English language before, *we want you to live a one-buttock life*.

Chapter 6

SHINING ON THE INSIDE

At your service...

How this chapter was invented …

The Scotsman: 'I think there needs to be something on healthy eating and exercise. It's really hard to shine on the outside if your innards are struggling.'

The Englishman [unconvinced]: 'That's not really our area. We're kinda happiness and positivity guys.'

The Scotsman [keen as English mustard]: 'We'd have to do a bit of learning. Just simple stuff about diet and guts and stuff.'

The Englishman: 'Gut bacteria! Are we really going to write a chapter on your intestines and poo, and shit?'

The Scotsman: 'Does pooing make you happy?'

The Englishman: 'Well, of course, but …'

The Scotsman: 'Then it needs a chapter.'

Toilet humour! *Bring it on …*

Health warning

We thought it would be deliciously ironic to start a chapter about health with a health warning. It's actually less of a warning and more about us playing our 'get out of jail free' card, so here goes …

> 'Life is like a box of chocolates. It doesn't last long if you're fat.'
> *Anon*

Please note: in the same way that Bono distanced himself from being shot by declaring that 'Sunday Bloody Sunday' was not a political song, this chapter is not anti-anything. To the ultra-sensitive, this section might seem harsh.

Please also note: if you scratch the surface, this section is pro everything. Pro-happiness, pro-people, pro-society, pro-common sense, pro-health, pro-fitness, pro-five-a-day, pro-sleep, pro-life and most of all pro-personal responsibility.

We are not monsters. We know people get ill and we understand that death is a major change of address.

On reflection, no need to play our 'get out of jail free' card, we'll save it for later. We've thrown a double. Onwards …

Spaced out

According to Mark Manson there's fitness. That's being able to run for the train.

There's wellness. That's rarely thinking, 'Jeez, I feel terrible'.

And there's super-wellness, aka shining. That's having focus, clarity, imagination, creativity, energy and resilience. An ability not just to get stuff done, but know which are the right things to get done. An ability to flip that which seems a blocker into a possibility. An unstoppable love of life and delight at having landed on one of the few rocks hurtling through the Universe with great music, fresh water and Netflix.

This chapter is dedicated to three facets of modern life that, if you get them right, will massively enhance your chances of shining on the *inside*. Once that's sorted, the shine leaks out of all your other orifices. Yes, just like the famous saying – sun really can shine out of it!

The three things are 'eat', 'move' and 'sleep'.[1]

Our opening gambit has us holding our hands up. We are experts in none of this, but here's our way in. In less than the blink of an evolutionary eye we've eradicated deficiency diseases, such as scurvy and rickets, and replaced them with excessivity diseases, such as heart disease and type 2 diabetes. Scarcity to abundance has happened a whole lot quicker than our brains can adapt to it.

Of course, this brand new world has opened the door for brand new diseases. Here's one of the new maladies in town: 'Depersonalization Disorder', sometimes known as DPD, which leaves sufferers feeling like they're not part of the world they live in.

'I feel spaced out a lot of the time. I feel like I'm not really here, like I'm living in a dream,' says DPD victim Michelle, a 22-year-old vlogger from London. 'I can't open my eyes wide enough or see things properly.'

---

[1] *Thank you to the wonderful Tom Rath. We highly recommend his book of the same name.*

DPD, a bona fide mental health disorder, can lead to severe depression as emotions, empathy and wellbeing give way to a detachment and distance from daily life.

'*I feel spaced out a lot of the time*' – safe to say, we've all had days like that. The prescription could have been that Michelle stops 'vlogging' (aka, sitting in front of a screen and recording videos of how shit her life is) and starts to get out more, maybe attend some social gatherings where she meets real people, interacts, makes some *real* friends, possibly falls in love and so on.

But no. Modern medicine tends not to work like that. Instead, Michelle's therapy is groundbreaking and snappily titled Transcranial Magnetic Stimulation (let's call it 'TMS'), in which she's fitted with what I would describe as a hovering helmet, an electromagnetic coil that sits a few inches above the targeted areas of her brain. Electromagnetic pulses are then generated that target the specific area of the brain thought to be causing the problem.

After completing her course of TMS, Michelle hasn't so far found any improvement, and is undertaking other treatment. In her own words: 'For me, I didn't find any difference, and that's difficult to talk about. But I think it needs more recognition and for people to know about it.'

So for 'groundbreaking' read 'doesn't actually work'. Michelle goes back to vlogging and the medical world scratches its collective cortex while it reflects on her disengagement with life. I'm sure you'll agree, spending all that time sitting in front a screen, interacting with a bunch of strangers, and yet somehow feeling disconnected from the world? It's most perplexing.

Sarcasm aside, we're not having a go at Michelle. Not really. If anything, it's a little dig at the medical profession who, in conjunction with the modern world of political correctness, continue to pussyfoot around a gaping chasm of the bleedin' obvious.

'I have no idea why I'm fat,' says man, 36, tucking into a box of Maltesers for his breakfast. Chain-smoking mother of four, Pauline, complains that she has to use food banks. I'm left wondering how on earth it can be that computer-games addict Nate from Gwent is depressed. Does anyone have any idea why the 18-hour-a-day workaholic from Manchester is on his third marriage, or why Derek, an astonishingly unfit middle-aged man, is on a cocktail of pills for blood pressure, diabetes and stress?

It's a real mind boggler.

The chump paradox

> Gaztelugatxe is an island off the coast of Spain that houses a church. The church has 230 steps to the top, and it's said that it's worth the climb.
>
> Gaztelugatxe can now mean, 'It's a lot of steps, but worth it.'
>
> What a great expression. The opposite of fast and easy, but worth every step of effort.

So why don't we change? If it's patently obvious that things are going awry, why do we continue to do them?

That's too big to sort in a chapter, but we'll do our best at reminding you of some common sense as well as introducing you to a bit of new info that we think will help.

The common wisdom in olden times (a couple of decades ago) was that after childhood the brain began the long process of decline; so when brain cells failed to develop properly, or were injured, or died, they could not be replaced.

The thinking was that since the brain could not change, human nature, which emerges from it, was necessarily fixed and unalterable as well.

That's a little bit true.

Late last century, there was a series of unexpected discoveries showing that the brain changed its very structure with each different activity it performed, perfecting its circuits so it was better suited to the task at hand. If certain 'parts' failed, then other parts could sometimes take over. The machine metaphor of the brain as an organ with specialized parts could not fully account for changes the scientists were seeing. They began to call this fundamental brain property 'neuroplasticity'.

It's a longish word, but fairly easy to grasp. Neuro is for 'neuron', the nerve cells in our brains and nervous systems. Plastic is for 'changeable, malleable, modifiable'. This term has slowly gained academic traction and begun to overturn the doctrine of the unchanging brain.

It was shown that children are not always stuck with the mental abilities they are born with; that the damaged brain can often reorganize itself so that when one part fails, another can come on as substitute; that if brain cells die, they can, at times, be replaced; that many circuits and even basic reflexes that we think are hardwired, are not. One scientist even showed that thinking, learning and acting can turn our genes on or off, thus shaping our brain anatomy, our behaviour and therefore our future (we'll be throwing more of that at you in a later chapter).

So plasticity is a good thing then? Well, sort of …

The plot thickens when we tell you there's also something called the 'plastic paradox', which goes some way to explaining the reason why people give up too early in any process of change. Your brain has developed grooves, like paths in a cornfield, where your thinking has created pathways of neurons. There's a saying: neurons that fire together, wire together. That pretty much sums it up.

New habits of thinking require effort. The neurons have to spark into life and create pathways as familiar as the old ones. Think about it. If you walk through the corn once, there's a bit of bent corn but not much else. Walk it 10 times and you can see the path that's been created. Walk it 1000 times and it's an established route. It's a lot easier for the brain to stick to a path it knows well, rather than create a new one.

The problem is that your brain has already developed some bad habits. These pathways aren't favourable, but you've thought the negative thoughts so long that they've become the easy route. Bottom line? Your brain doesn't do what's best, it does what's easiest.

Not being familiar with the way the brain changes, people are discouraged by little or no progress. Seemingly having to fight an uphill battle with no end in sight, they surrender prematurely. Therefore, in order not to be defeated by insufficient knowledge, let's explore this particular principle of change in greater detail.

The plastic paradox refers to the apparently contradictory effects of plasticity: on the one hand, the plasticity of the brain enables us to create new patterns of behaviour until old age. But on the other hand, the same plasticity makes the brain rigid, resisting change and holding on to old habits.

You have to imagine the brain as a faithful servant. Let's call it your 'inner Jeeves'. In principle, it serves us well and has only our wellbeing in mind. But, like any butler who has been in service for a long time, the brain thinks it knows us better than we know ourselves. It is not easily convinced if one day, out of the blue, we decide to take up a new habit. If you announce to yourself, 'I'm joining a gym and will be going every day', your inner Jeeves will be saying, '*That's a jolly big change. Why don't you just go for a day or two, and then when you wake up with aching limbs on day three, you can give up?*'

Or you decide, 'I'm eating healthily. That's seven fruit and veg portions a day, no red meat and a ban on alcohol.' Your inner Jeeves knows better. He'll have a little chuckle. '*Very amusing sir. I'd suggest you do it for today but there's a work do tomorrow night so you can let it slip. In fact, haven't you pre-ordered a sirloin, rare? And there will be Prosecco.*'

Your inner Jeeves thinks any deviation from the norm is another of your follies and resists the change. Hence, it's a real challenge to persist at something new until it's grooved in as a new habit and Jeeves gets on board.

Bottom line? There's effort involved in personal change. Your job is to be assertive with yourself. (Lest you forget, in our witty butler metaphor, 'Jeeves' is, in fact, you!)

It can be a proper internal fist fight. In the blue corner is you, and in the red corner it's you again! Change means you have to regain the upper hand and straighten out who serves whom. Your brain is prepared to learn and change over time, albeit reluctantly. It usually gives in when it repeatedly receives 'commands' from us over a considerable period of time.

In other words, we have to make use of repetition to win over our brain. At some point there will be a moment when the new 'behaviour-to-be' becomes a power in its own right. After having been repeated, the new, implemented habit demands to be repeated for its own sake. That is the moment when the uphill battle is over because now the new habit is working in your favour. While at the beginning you have to push-start it to get it on its way, later on you will be pulled to pursue it by its own power.

There are plenty of examples. Gym membership spikes in January and falls back by February. But those still going by March will go forever because Jeeves wouldn't ever let you slump back into feeling lethargic, overweight and baggy-bellied. Whereas Jeeves would previously have used a couple of work nights in a hotel as an excuse for no exercise, he now searches the internet for a hotel with a gym. Unthinkable, compared to three months ago, but Jeeves rather likes the new you.

Check out Gav's story below. It's a beautiful example of Jeeves in action.

Free honks to keep you going

Two years ago I took up running and quickly discovered that bad knees and walking like you'd shat yourself were small prices to pay for the upside of the 'runner's high' – weight loss, stress reduction, enhanced energy, better sleep and endorphin-fuelled glee.

One of the reasons I felt the need to do something was an interview I read online with a renowned business speaker who said, *'You can't trust a fat motivational speaker'*. He had a point. If I can't motivate me to look after me, then what gives me the right to stand up and tell others to inspire or embrace positive change in their own lives?

> 'If you only *do one thing* today, please breathe. More people die a year from not breathing than almost any other cause.'
>
> *Philip Ardagh*

I wasn't exactly fat, but I was overweight and incredibly unfit. Now I'm not a natural long-distance runner, I played a huge amount of sport as a kid but it was all sports like rugby, tennis and volleyball. Basically, sports that require you to run for a short time and then stop for a break!

Long distances, with no tea-shop? I'm more Phoebe from 'Friends' than Mo Farah! Nonetheless I have persisted with it. The health benefits are just too great and too fun to ignore.

But I had to start small. I couldn't even run round the block and, trust me, our block is really rather tiny. In fact, if I'm being honest, I couldn't even run to the end of the road. I gave myself a fright. Despite Jeeves telling me not to, I stuck at it.

I entered a 5k. Jeeves told me I was being an idiot. I kind of agreed. The goal was simply to finish. This I did. Middle finger to Jeeves.

I upped myself to 10k – the goal being to run the whole thing in under 75 minutes without walking. This I did, in less than an hour. My stamina was building. I had momentum. Jeeves was impressed.

I upgraded again, this time to a half marathon. That meant training four times a week and adding in a hilly session. The goal was just to finish without walking. Curses; I finished, but found myself walking around the 10-mile mark. Jeeves told me I'd made the rookie mistake of going out too fast too early. He patted me on the back and kept me going. Jeeves was finally on my side.

The only natural next step up from a half marathon is, of course, the full 26.2 miles. I think it might even have been Jeeves' idea. I figured that if you're going to run a marathon, then you might as well run the most famous one in the world. A trip to London beckoned. Jeeves loves London.

The London Marathon is, to this day, one of the most positive, uplifting and inspiring experiences of my entire life. Which is weird, because it's also the most painful. Not just in the obvious places, like feet and knees, but friction of the inner thighs and extreme nipple rub. Just kidding, I was wearing Nip-Eaze nipple protectors.

Sure, Jesus sprinted past me on the final 100 metres and I was beaten by a Tyrannosaurus Rex, but I'm not sure I'll ever experience anything again that can compare to the euphoria of finishing.

Four and a half hours gives you plenty of time to reflect. I was pounding the pavement with 40 000 people, each and every one running for a reason. A positive reason. Running with a purpose. Whether that is to win, set a new PB, to have fun, to raise money for a charity, to raise awareness of something meaningful, remember a loved one or to support a loved one, *everyone* was running in the same direction with purpose. (Apart from the guy who ran backwards. Although technically he was still moving in the same direction.)

Elite athletes aside, no one was competing against each other. Quite the opposite. Runners were encouraging each other, helping, supporting, stopping to check on those struggling in the heat and some literally carrying complete strangers over the finish line.

Then there's the crowd. I have no idea how many people line the streets for the London Marathon but it sure felt like millions. Millions of complete strangers, each and every one there for a reason. A positive reason. A purpose. Whether that was to have fun, support a charity, to raise awareness of something meaningful, remember a loved one or to support a loved one running, *everyone* was cheering with purpose.

At about 16 miles I spotted a spectator holding a fishing rod. Hanging on the end was a horn, one of those proper old-fashioned horns that you have to honk. Attached was a sign that read, '*Free honks to keep you going*'. And boy did I honk that horn. And yes, it kept me going; it made me smile and my energy lifted yet again.

And this was the big takeaway for me. It seemed that at every moment I began to slow, struggle or hurt – and trust me there were many – there was someone or something in place to lift my spirits. It all came from people and their kindness, their humour, their creativity and energy.

My marathon journey was spread out over two years and the vast majority of this was solitary 4am starts pounding the streets of Edinburgh for hours on end. Jeeves thought I was bonkers, but I didn't listen to his advice about staying in bed. The goal was simple, run the London Marathon. Time didn't matter, just finish and don't be the guy who dies.

I finished and I didn't die. In fact, I felt more alive than I ever have.

I still run. In fact, Jeeves won't let me *not* run!

Grub's up

Andy recently read about a new kind of diet, the 'berry and porcupine' favoured by the nomadic Hazda tribe of northern Tanzania. They have fabulous digestive systems which contribute to good immunity and, whereas heart disease is the number one killer in western Europe, nobody dies from heart disease in the Hazdas. We're talking nobody, *ever!* What's more, they have zero (I repeat, ZERO) cases of Alzheimer's.

So what's cracking off with the Hazdas?

Microbes, you see. Their super-wellness starts off inside their guts. The nomadic nature of Hazdas means they don't have possessions, or fridges, or shops. Yes, in another sentence that's never been written before, the Hazdas have no Asda. On a daily basis they eat what they can catch, or what's on the bushes. Hence, a balanced mixture of berries and porcupines. Some grubs too, apparently. To quote from the article I read, the Hazdas are 'always hungry but never starving'. Plus, very importantly, they eat socially, as a group.

Which brings us to another rather big 'so what'?

The basic structure of human beings is hunter–gatherer. Not that long ago, and with the Hazdas it's still the case, life was active. You were born on the move. Nowadays we're living in offices in front of screens, hunting information, gathering coffee and sugar. That's created a mismatch between how your body is designed and the environment it's designed for.

The availability of everything without moving your heavyweight backside off your seat creates an obesogenic world in which it's very easy to get fat. Please note: it's easy but not inevitable.

Whereas our 'Happy Meals' start in a queue after which a one-star trainee asks you if you want to 'go large with that', the Hazdas' starts by preparing them from scratch. In a world in which our 'Happy Meals' come with a cheap plastic toy, or a scary clown, the Hazda's 'happy meal' is one where everyone sits down, at the same time, at the same table and eats just enough in a happy atmosphere.

Some scientists managed to persuade the Hazda men to wear heart rate monitors. The result? Wowza again. It seems that their routine of lots of moderate activity, brisk walking mostly (and this continues into old age) is conducive to a wonderful heartbeat. The conclusion from the University of Arizona research is that your body, your heart in particular, WANTS to be worked.

We tend to forget that we're the first generation in the history of humans to be over-fed but under-nourished. This stems partly from marketing. Healthy food is nicely behaved. Carrots don't shout, appear on prime-time TV adverts or make bold claims, they just sit there, in the veg aisle, scrubbed up, doing their best to look orangey. Ditto radishes and runner beans, the only difference being purply and greeny.

All the unhealthy food shouts loudly. It's ironic that the ADHD food behaves as if it's infected with the very affliction it causes. The sugary cereals are screaming that they've got 30% reduced sugar or they've been pepped with added vitamins. *'Look at us. We're fortified!'* They're shaking their fists and bulging their biceps as you pass by. *'We'll show you how to start your day … on a sugary high.'*

So, are we suggesting you up your levels of porcupine and pineapple? Or move your family to northern Tanzania? Not really. We hope you'll get our wider point about movement, sufficiency and healthy guts.

There's a problem with the Hazdas you see. With such healthy microbes, you'd think the Hazdas would experience longevity, but no. The reason they *never* die from heart disease is the same as why they haven't ever had a case of Alzheimer's – because they never live long enough, what with lions, snakes and packs of wild dogs.

Berries and porcupines? On balance, I'll stick to Asda. But the healthy aisle.

Here are our modern-day rules for eating properly, staying slim and living forever.

- Don't eat anything out of a packet.
- Don't eat in front of a screen or standing up.
- Don't eat without cutlery or out of a box.
- Don't eat anything delivered to your door by a man on a motorbike.
- Don't eat anything passed to you in your car through a hatch.
- Plus, do not eat anything your great grandma would not have recognized as food.

Guaranteed lottery win

Whoever invented the day made a huge error. Twenty-four hours might have been okay back in the day when the day was invented, but it doesn't fit modern life. We're cramming so much in that something

'Slept like a log, woke up on fire.'
Unknown

has to spill out and that something is quite often sleep. Let me guess, you think that trimming a few hours here and there is fine because you'll catch up at the weekend, or on holiday, or when you're dead – whichever comes first?

Sleep doesn't really work like that. If you keep trimming your sleep time, death might come quicker than you think. Or certainly burn-out, panic attacks and your Irritable Bastard Syndrome will flare up.

We have both feet in the real world. Lack of kip during the week and binge sleeping at the weekend is sometimes necessary. But it's not a great long-term strategy. Your body likes regular patterns of enoughness. That's enough hours and decent quality.

A University of Warwick study analysed the sleep patterns of more than 30 500 people in UK households across four years, finding that improving your sleep quality leads to levels of mental and physical health comparable to those of somebody who's won a jackpot of around £200,000. Further, quality of sleep is more important than quantity for optimal health and happiness. They also cited numerous wellbeing benefits (calmer, better able to deal with stress, lower blood pressure), concluding that working on better sleep could be an effective, cheap and simple public health strategy

---

Definition

Ultracrepidarianist: the habit of giving opinions and advice outside of one's knowledge or competence.

On the whole, we're anti it.

Look, we're not claiming to be sleep experts. You already know the secrets of getting a good night's kip, so we're not going to trot them out. The same principle applies as for eating and exercising, it's not lack of knowledge, it's commitment to making the changes that hampers us.

Your health and vitality are your gifts to the world. If getting more sleep is equivalent to a lottery win, we suggest you treat yourself and your family to a guaranteed winning ticket.

What have the Mexicans ever done for us? Or the South Africans come to think of it

Life's like a massive Mexican stand-off. You're staring at life and life is staring back.

Who's gonna blink first?

We're telling you straight, it's not going to be life. Life isn't going to back down. In fact, if you're waiting for life to back down, for that perfect moment to change, you'll need a lot more than one measly lifetime. *You've* got to change.

Rather than copying everyone else's strategy of 'doing the same but faster' (look around you, does it seem to be working?) maybe the secret is to be comfortable with what you already have.

Of course, that takes courage. That moreish race is a real bastard to leave. Are we really expecting you to kick off your running shoes and watch the Joneses disappear out of sight?

So to finish, here's some thinking for you. Andy spent a week working in South Africa, which he describes as a heady mix of lovely people, sunshine and massive social problems.

Landing at Joburg, he boarded their swanky 'Gautrain' that transported him into the business district of Sandton. From the plushness of his air-conditioned carriage, he watched the shanty towns sweep by.

So let's play a game. Let's invite one of the township ladies back to your house. Someone who walks four miles to work and who lives in a shack. Someone who shares her one-bed, tin-roofed abode with her husband and four children. *'Come on in and wipe your calloused feet. Crikey that's one helluva dirty jumper you're wearing. Let me stick it in my washing machine. Sit down on my comfy sofa while I turn on the satellite TV. Do you want a cup of tea? And lookie here, in my fridge, enough chilled food to last you several months. And at bedtime I'll give you my spare room. Yes, we have a bedroom each plus an extra room, just for visitors, with a soft bed and a fluffy pillow. And the best thing of all, hot and cold water from the taps and a flushing toilet (well, two actually, one upstairs and one downstairs for convenience). And tomorrow you can come to my place of work and have a look around. It's an office, with computers, and at lunch we eat in the staff restaurant.'*

What would your guest say, apart from *'You lucky git!'*

And, most poignantly, what advice would they give you? We suspect it would be something along the lines of *'You have everything and more. Savour it. Appreciate what you have and take it easy. Enjoy your work but make sure you spend time with your family. You have enough money, so stop chasing more stuff. Enjoy the experience. Eat healthily. Keep moving.*

And sleep well.'

Chapter 7
THE SHINE TOP 10

It's interesting to consider that you don't drown from falling in the water. *You drown from staying there.*

You're more than halfway into the book. Sniff the air. Go on, do it. You'll detect a whiff of passion. We're going to reward you with some quick wins: 10 easy-peasy do-able strategies that will massively increase your chances of shining.

We're calling them our #SHINE10. If you stick with our 'falling in water' analogy, these are 10 rubber rings. Grab them and haul yourself out.

A word before the off – just because they're do-able, doesn't mean people are actually doing them. Just because they're simple, doesn't mean they're easy. And just because they might be a bit odd, doesn't make them silly.

We've avoided the usual array of self-help triteness. What follows is an eclectic gaggle of techniques and philosophies from around the world. We're off to Japan, Finland, Denmark, Madras and Scotland. You can expect cricket, plot twists and to live a full-ass life.

But first, a wee bit of magic …

Ordinary magic

That you only live once is, of course, a lie. You only die once. You live every single day.

But sometimes it doesn't feel like that. There are times when the normal rough and tumble of life becomes a right kicking.

Resilience applies to hearts and minds as well as bones and skin. If you cut yourself, it scabs over, starts itching and when the scab falls off there's a brand new piece of you underneath. You've grown some new skin.

Ditto if you break a leg; it hurts, but within a few weeks your bones have knitted back together, strong as before. Crikey, that's clever.

Emotions work on the same principle. If you lose a loved one, boy does it hurt. Worse than a broken leg. Marriage break up? Ouch, that takes a while to scab over. But your emotional band aid system will eventually heal you.

So, here's something that you might not be expecting from a book about happiness: being sad is an important part of being happy. Applied to the concept of SHINE, it's okay to have your glow dimmed a bit, sometimes. Full wattage is not always possible. It's ok to feel shit. A life of euphoric happiness would be bizarre. Lows are inevitable. Welcome them. Let an occasional bad day into your life, show it around, then show it the door.

Pain is an inextricable thread in the fabric of life. To tear it out is not only impossible but destructive, because everything else unravels too. It's part of life that has made you who you are. Nulling it with meds means you don't learn from it. You don't emerge stronger, and so next time strife attacks you (which it is sure to do) you'll wilt.

When it comes to pain, you can run but you can't hide. It's not, 'What happens' but 'What happens next?' Sometimes there's no alternative but to sit down and have a huge sob. Crying serves a purpose. It lets stuff out. It shows the world you're hurt. And it's the start of the repairing process. It's messy! It's your safety valve.

> 'I play all my Country and Western music backwards — your lover returns, your dog comes back, and you cease to be an alcoholic.'
>
> Linda Smith

We all possess what's called 'ordinary magic'; time heals all ills, it's true.

So here's a new word for you: *sisu*, Finnish for the psychological strength that allows a person to overcome extraordinary challenges. *Sisu* is similar to what we might call perseverance, or the trendier concept of grit, it connotes both determination and bravery, a willingness to act even when the reward seems out of reach.

Sisu, ordinary magic, grit, bravery, resilience … it all points to developing a backbone instead of a wishbone.

There's a certain boldness about being able to stare catastrophe in the face and flick your middle finger back at it. Here are a few ideas that will help with that middle finger salute.

SHINE #1: 'Plot twist!'

You are a story teller. Not just you, all humans are. Stories are what link us to our ancestors and to those who don't yet exist.

We have stories about everything. Your inner story is one of the great classics, although only in your own head. Here's a dirty little secret – you can tell a different and better story. In fact, a change to your inner story is the fastest way to a better you.

Of course, in the story of your life, you are the central character. Everything is told in first person. You are well versed in your own story, telling it to yourself every day.

And don't we just love a tragedy! If you're not careful, problems loom large and they can dominate your backstory. They become well-rehearsed tales, magnified and re-lived every time you tell them. It's astonishingly easy to become the victim. Bad things always happen to you, right?

But, of course, you're the author. It's your life and your story. You might not be able to change the events that have happened, but you can re-cast yourself as the hero. That changes how you view the past and, spookily, will affect how you approach the future.

Our first shiny strategy is therefore a bit tongue in cheek (but only a little bit) – it's to change your language. In the same way that, in the 1980s, 'problems' became 'challenges', we'd like you to start saying, '*Plot twist!*'

So when something doesn't go according to plan, it's not a nightmare, crisis, challenge or problem, it's merely a plot twist.

Shout It out. Rejoice! All good stories have a plot twist, an unexpected turn of events that nobody saw coming. Some books have several. Your life is a story. Plot twists are inevitable. They're there to make things more interesting.

Our clincher? A good life is not a life without plot twists. A good life is a life with *good* plot twists. Therefore, if you want to graduate to the status of Happiness Grand Master, you have to start appreciating your plot twists. The turbulence, challenges, strains, sadness, disasters and faux pas. They're inevitable. Smile and be grateful for them.

Plot twists! Woo Hoo. They exist because you're alive.

SHINE #2: Live a full-ass life

Our second shiny strategy is a risky one.

Dostoyevsky's words are true, but comforting. 'Pain and suffering are always inevitable for a large intelligence and a deep heart.' What he means is those who care the most are more likely to suffer the most. The ones at work who are off with stress (real stress, not the self-made fake stuff) are invariably the ones who care.

> 'I hate my supervisor. Behind her desk it says "You don't have to be mad to work here, but it helps". Mind you, she's written it in her own shit.'
> *Alan Carr*

The ones who can't be bothered have inoculated themselves against real stress. If you don't give a monkey's about work, customers or your colleagues, you will survive the rough and tumble just fine. But your lack of caring also means you're missing out on the really good stuff – passion, energy, purpose, drive, vigour – all the things that tally with that precious gift of being alive.

It's as though there's a botheredness spectrum. There's an argument that you can, perhaps, care too much, a sort of 'extreme botheredness' that might end up destroying you. The best teachers, doctors, nurses, police and tax collectors suffer from this. If they can't do their job properly, it pains them. Their passion flares up and their botheredness destroys them, like a microwaved jacket potato, from the inside out.

So, although it's true that you can be *too bothered*, we'd argue it's a much better place than the other end of the botheredness spectrum – the apathetic 'don't give a shit' end is a dire place.

These are the un-dead. There's a faint pulse as they go about their daily routine, slouching from meeting to meeting, grumbling in the corridors and moaning about the traffic without realizing they are the traffic. The problem with the grumble brigade is that it's an easy habit to sink into.

Apathy doesn't just seep in at work. It can leak into your life. You can chunter along, fuelled by low-level grumbling.

Thus, our top tip is don't half-ass anything. Whatever you do, always use your full ass.

It takes effort to be your best self. *Get bothered*. The risk is that you end up caring too much and run the stress risk. On balance, we're keen that you reposition yourself at the 'give a damn' end of the botheredness spectrum.

It's a risk worth taking.

SHINE #3: Let it go

We've all been wronged, treated unfairly, dissed, dismissed, abused and upset. As someone once said to me, 'I haven't got time for any new wounds – my old wounds are still healing.'

> 'Life is very short, as there's no time for fussing and fighting, my friend.'
>
> *The Beatles*

It's time to let it all go and move on because, guess what, the world has finished with your past if you have.

When you forgive, you in no way change the past – but you sure do change the future. Inability to forgive means you are holding onto the past – you are punishing yourself! Forgiveness is, first and foremost, for your benefit. It means recognizing that you've already been hurt once. You need to let go from this form of mental self-harm.

For example, I once ran a course and a guy said, vehemently I might add, that there's no way he could be happy because his dad had ruined his life. Summing his life story up, it seems that his dad walked out on his mum, leaving her to bring him and his brother up. His mum struggled and ended up depressed. He now looks after his mum. He's an angry man, and it's all his dad's fault.

It's not difficult to see exactly what he means. That's a tough story and his dad walking out certainly triggered a dire train of events. It was a massive plot twist. But this was 30 years ago! And remember that each time you tell your story, you are re-living it in the present, so one of the most fruitful options is to learn to change your story. Change your story to one that says how you made the courageous choice to let go, forgive and learn from what happened and how the experience of adversity has made you a better and stronger person. In his case, he could choose to tell the story of how he gave up his job to look after his poorly mum. It's your story, so why not be your own hero? It lets go of a bit of mental clutter and clears some space for happiness.

> **Top tip:**
>
> Be good to people. Even the shitty ones. Let the assholes be assholes, you'll sleep better.
>
> Gav

Carrying a grievance is like carrying a hand grenade that's superglued to your hand. It keeps blowing up in your face. You may well have been hurt in a relationship or had a horrible boss, been bullied at school or been done for speeding twice in two days, but seething about it and carrying a grudge?

Ask yourself, who exactly are you hurting with that grudge?

Be kind to yourself. Let go. Forgiveness is for you, not them! If you want any more persuading, this should do it, the words of holocaust survivor Eva Kor: 'I forgive the Nazis not because they deserve it but because I deserve it.'

Eva Kor, ladies and gentlemen. *Amen.*

SHINE #4: Shine-tinted specs

Everyone knows and understands déjà vu, that feeling of familiarity, an experience that has happened to you before. Very few know the opposite, vujà dé, which is when we see a familiar situation through new eyes.

Rose-tinted spectacles are sooooo last millennium. We're offering you an upgrade to 'shine-tinted'. Not only will they help with your vujà dé, they also allow you to illuminate wonderful experiences that most people miss.

First, the science bit. I'm not sure the missing link was the jump from monkeys to humans. I think that was a slow process of evolution where each generation painstakingly passed on a slightly bigger brain. This information processing power has then allowed us to hit the gas pedal of evolution, so while our old mates the Congolese Bonobo continue to swing through the trees, we've accelerated away, evolving into the kings of the swingers.

Natural selection put happiness at the back of the queue, which leaves humans with an evolutionary hangover. 'Negativity bias' is an unfortunate neurological adaptation that has kept our species alive and thriving but also keeps many of us in a constant state of irritation and stress.

Your attention is a bit like a 1980s vacuum cleaner. I remember my gran's eyes lighting up as she showed me her new 'hoover' (this was PD – *Pre-Dyson* – when they were all called 'hoovers') that had a light on it. 'So you can see into the corners,' she said, her eyes lighting up brighter than her new head-lamped device.

Anyhow, your attention is like a combination of a spotlight and a vacuum cleaner. Whatever your attention is on is lit up and sucked into your brain.

If you don't take charge of your experiences, your brain will do it on autopilot. Your brain cannot NOT do it! If left to itself, your brain will suck up all the negativity. It is tuned into danger, problems and deficiency, your antennae ever alert for bad stuff.

This links to memory. Think of your memory as a vast warehouse. The person in charge of retrieval (i.e. you) has to find a way of storing each memory. If you alphabeticized them, your recall of aardvarks would be superb but you'd forget what a zebra was. You, the memory keeper, invented a dual-recording system; firstly, we code them according to power, but – and this is the clever but unfortunate bit – bad ones are stored right at the front of the warehouse. That means really powerful bad memories are right there, at the door. Your most traumatic and painful experiences sting like a hot iron, branded indelibly into your emotions with a burning, 'What an utter dick I am' or 'How terrible is my life' motif.

The really fabulous stuff can only be accessed when you've clambered past the boxes and boxes and boxes of shit.

Hence, onto our tip. Look through shine-tinted specs and you'll see past the rubbish. Your new vision will pick out the really good stuff that's sometimes right under your nose. Once you've noticed it, suck it up, savour it and store it in an easy-to-remember place.

Please note, your shine-tinted glasses don't mean you're denying or resisting the bad, you're merely acknowledging and savouring the good. You're learning to be aware of the whole truth and nothing but the truth: that there is oodles of wonderful stuff out there and you're going to damn well spot and savour it.

Plus, by taking in the good, you learn to feel a whole lot better, more vital, and are therefore better able to deal with the bad.

SHINE #5: Celebrate stuff that didn't happen

An advanced version of tilting towards the good. Have you ever asked yourself, *'What hasn't happened that I didn't want that I haven't celebrated?'*

Thought not!

Sadly, unless you're a black belt happiness ninja, your mind doesn't sit in traffic thinking how lucky you are to have a car. It curses the late meeting instead of rejoicing that you have a job. It tuts at the crumbs on the worktop instead of being grateful you've got (on the whole) wonderful children.

The opposite of savouring good experiences is to notice the many things that could have gone badly but didn't. Hence, *what hasn't happened that you didn't want that you haven't celebrated?*

I woke up and didn't have toothache. I got to work without crashing my car. I haven't got diabetes. My children aren't poorly. I haven't just stubbed my toe ...

Of course, it's hard to notice something that *didn't* happen. But it's helpful to switch your thinking to what I'm right this minute trademarking as 'neo-Stoic'™, the definition of which I'm stating as, *'Thinking about all the bad things that could have happened, but didn't. And then celebrating the positive result.'*

Have a go, it's fabulous fun. In fact, it's one of those mental muscles that gets stronger the more you exercise it. We'll get you warmed up, and then you can write your own list of bad stuff that hasn't happened that you haven't celebrated.

Here are your starters ... the accident you didn't have, the power cut that never happened, the headache you didn't suffer, the supermarket queue that wasn't there, the lack of red traffic lights on the way home, the train that wasn't delayed ...

1

2

3

4

5

6

7

8

9

10

SHINE #6 Scratch your itch

Next up, Japan. Via Scotland.

Gav quit his 'proper job' after attending a workshop called 'Putting the Fun Back in the Staffroom'.

You can imagine the enthusiasm when we were all told we *must* attend this workshop. It would be more of the same patronising rubbish that we'd heard a million times before presented by someone who has never even done what we do. I couldn't have been more wrong.

> 'Don't ask what the world needs. Ask what makes you come alive and do that ... because what the world really needs is people who have come alive.'
>
> *Howard W. Thurman*

I laughed, I learned, I was inspired, I was challenged and most of all, I was moved. Moved to change career.

'If you hate your job,' the speaker began, 'I have some ground-breaking advice for you.' I straightened up in my seat, listening for the sage advice. 'Leave. Go away. Get a smile back on your face, let everyone else get on with what they love to do and go find something that makes you happy. Something that makes you come alive.'

I sat there, looking around me at my colleagues, thinking, 'Wow, she should leave, her over there, she should go, he definitely needs to go.' I sat there picking people off.

I had to stop myself. Today hadn't been about them. It wasn't about how they behave, how they act or the impact they have or don't have. Today had been all about me and just me. How I choose to think, how I choose to feel, how I choose to act and behave. It was all about the impact I choose to have in the world. And that's what this chapter is all about. You and all the choices that make you come alive.

> 'If you end up with a boring, miserable life because you listened to you mom, your dad, your teacher, your priest, or some guy on television telling you how to do your shit, then you deserve it.'
>
> Frank Zappa

I handed in my notice the very next day.

I had to go home and tell my wife-to-be that I had quit my job. Was she angry or concerned? Nope, she was delighted! I had slowly been turning into one of THEM. 'Them' who come home every day and share with their nearest and dearest all that went wrong, could go wrong and nearly went wrong – the entire back-catalogue of their day's lowlights exaggerated in excruciating detail.

My wife Ali is nothing like this. She comes home every single day and tells me something extraordinary. I am utterly convinced that every single day my wife – in her way – changes the world. In fact, I can remember when we first met 20 years ago in our first year at university. Ali came home from her first ever day of her first ever teaching placement. And as she stood there sharing her day with everyone, I couldn't help but think, 'Wow, who are you? You've just changed the world.' I think Ali has Poppins' blood.

I started out my career in the same way, but somewhere along the way I forgot my purpose, I lost my why.

There are millions of people all across the world who wake up every morning before work with a feeling of dread in the pit of their stomachs, what Guy Browning calls 'minor glumness' which, if untreated, can manifest as 'Irritable Bastard Syndrome'.

> 'Life doesn't give us purpose. We give life purpose.'
> *The Flash*

We all need that something special, a reason to get out of bed in the morning. It's the cape. What's your cape? Think of the cape as your purpose, your why. You can survive without it, but with it you fly.

Many have the cape, some even put it on. The flying part? That's the difficult bit.

The Japanese call it your *ikigai*. Andy calls it your energy transfusion.

Ikigai is pronounced 'itchy-guy'. And we want you to scratch that itch. Your itchy-guy is your drive, your purpose, the reason you get up in the morning.

Your *ikigai* lies at the centre of those interconnecting circles. If you are lacking in one area, it is said you are missing out on your life's potential. Not only that, but you are missing out on your chance to live a long and happy life.

The term *ikigai* is composed of two Japanese words: *iki* referring to life, and *gai*, which roughly means 'the realization of what one expects and hopes for'.

It's important to note that *ikigai* is not necessarily linked to one's economic status or the present state of society. Even in difficult times when we may feel our shine is somewhat dimmed, but we have a goal in mind, we may feel *ikigai*. Behaviours that make us feel *ikigai* are not actions we are forced to take – these are free choices. Natural and spontaneous ones at that.

While *ikigai* is familiar to most Japanese, it's a whole new way of thinking for most and it can take time. The Japanese believe it's worth taking the time for.

When was the last time you took some time out to really think about your *ikigai*?

Take a moment to draw your own version of the overlapping circles of the *ikigai* symbol and consider the four initial questions. Bear in mind the questions and the answers can be overlapping, in some profound ways, and all four questions must be answered in order to develop a clear sense of one's *ikigai*.

What do you love?

What aspects of your life make you come alive and give you your shine? What's your passion? What would you do if you didn't have to make money, if you could just follow your heart?

What are you great at?

What unique skills do you have that come most naturally to you? This should be easy to answer and less emotional than the first question. What talents have you cultivated and what do you excel at even when you aren't trying?

What does the world need from you?

This is more difficult to answer. What's your cause? Your mission? What hurts your heart or moves you? What change would you most love to create in the world? What would you give your life for? As the New Zealand All Blacks would say, 'Plant trees you'll never see.'

What do people value and pay you for?

What service, value or offering do you bring, or could you bring, that brings real value to others? Something people need and are happy to pay for or share some value in exchange.

Think of your *ikigai* as the greatest jigsaw puzzle of all time. You definitely need the big picture to help you. It's still difficult and it takes time, but when all the pieces fit together, it's pure magic.

We all know it's not easy to live with only a few pieces of life's puzzle in place. It's incredibly frustrating, irritating and unfulfilling.

Imagine how much time we collectively waste on stuff that doesn't matter.

When working out your *ikigai*, make the effort and give it the time it deserves. It boils down to this: working hard for something we don't care about is called stress. Working hard for something we love is called passion.

SHINE #7: Be Chris Tavare

You can become hyper-sensitive to what others say about you. Sometimes it's the smallest things that end up upsetting you. To help you roll with the punches, here's a super-cool analogy and wonderfully refreshing activity …

First, chill. Have you ever accidentally worded things rather badly and said something that, on reflection, might have sounded harsh? We have too! And others have done it to us. The result is that a misjudged comment has caused more upset than it was worth.

Next time someone says something that would normally cause you to bristle and react, let it go. Choose not to respond. Think of life like a cricket test match. For our foreign readers, cricket is the ultimate in civilization. It's gloriously slow, bordering on tedious, with the players breaking for afternoon tea. The game itself involves a bowler throwing a rock-hard ball at a batter, whose job is to hit the ball and run as fast as they can. There are some nuances and technicalities, but that's basically it.

The reason it's so slow is that the batter doesn't hit every single ball. Some balls are too fast, too slow, too wide or unplayable. So, more often than not the batter will let the ball go, and it sails through the wicket-keeper, who catches it and polishes it as the bowler saunters 100 yards back to their starting point. And off we go again …

That happens for five days and it usually ends in a draw.

Andy's proper old, so he remembers an English batsman called Chris Tavare. In a game of slowness, Chris was the slowest.

He somehow carved a career out of letting almost every single ball go through to the wicket-keeper. In the summer of 1981, I was glued to the TV as Chris took nearly seven hours to score a measly 35 runs in Madras. Ladies and gents, it was mesmerizing. Compelling. Achingly slow. A news report described his performance thus; 'He began not to bat but to set, concrete drying under the sun.'

Anyhow, when you choose *not* to rise to a misjudged comment, think of yourself as letting that one go through to the wicket-keeper. To win the game, the batter doesn't have to slog every ball, and to maintain your sanity and serenity, you don't have to rise to every comment. Let it pass. Life's too short. Stop trying to beat the hell out of everyone and everything.

Be Chris Tavare.

But sometimes criticism can really sting. And there are plenty of people who stand on the edges of life, throwing negativity around. Social media makes this ever so easy. Amazon reviews doubly so!

People whose opinions I genuinely value ...

The trick is to ignore the criticism, unless it's delivered by someone you truly respect and care for. And who cares for you too. In which case, the criticism will be well intended.

From now on, the only criticism that you will accept is that delivered by those you respect and/or those whose opinion you value. Think about that inner circle of people – there won't be many. You should be able to write their names in the postage-stamp-sized box.

Next time someone says something bad, cruel or upsetting, check if their name is in the box. If not, you can ignore the comment because their opinion doesn't count. If their name is in the box, act on their words. They care about you, so take measures to improve yourself.

SHINE #8: Plenty of the f-word

About time we had some poetry don't you think? Here's a little ditty by Piet Hein:

> 'The road to wisdom?
> Well, it's plain and simple to express:
> Err and err and err again
> but less and less and less.'

Makes sense. The road to wisdom is to mess up again and again, but gradually less so.

Which brings us to the f-word. *Failure.* Dirty, rotten, foul-mouthed, despicable failure.

'Failure', which is often harder to drop into a conversation than the phrase 'donkey sodomy'. But we do need failure. Not failure the result: losing the business, losing the relationship, failing the interview. But failure the process: learning, improving, iterating, removing slack, becoming lean, becoming fighting-fit, installing effectiveness, getting really really good, broadening, widening, gaining wisdom, picking yourself up and smiling and trying once again. Yeah, that.

The whole process of succeeding requires lots and lots of the f-word. And we don't like it: we want approval, we want love, we want accolades. But hang on a minute; no, you don't. You really want to grow, you really want to discover who the heck you are, you really want to see just what your limits are. You want to start creating your personal best. If you want to shine, you will have to accept abject failure. Repeatedly. With tears at times. With jeers at others.

Failure, yes. But stay in the game.

The truth is simple: if we're unwilling to fail, we're unwilling to succeed.

SHINE #9: Get snuggly

Us Brits, we like to moan about our weather. It's a bit of a hobby of ours. Personally, I love our seasons, especially summer. It's my favourite day of the year.

So, because our weather's a bit dodgy, we holiday in Greece and Florida, or buy a holiday home in sunny Spain.

The world happiness league tables suggest we might be missing a trick. At the time of writing, the UK is languishing at 17th in the international league table of happiness, casting our envious eyes north. The top five have all got weather that's worse than ours. So what is it about the Scandis? How on earth can you be cold and happy?

The secret to happiness seems to be in embracing the snuggles. Here's a raft of new words for you; we think you'll notice a theme:

Mysa. [Swedish] To be engaged in a pleasant or comfortable activity; to be content or comfortable; to get cosy; to snuggle up.

Peiskos. [Norwegian] Lit. Fireplace coziness, sitting in front of a crackling fireplace enjoying the warmth.

Hygge. [Danish] Enjoying life's simple pleasures. Coziness. Snuggliness.

All the above are more than words, they're philosophies. The most famous is Denmark's *hygge*. I love it because it's primitive and basic, like me. You can't buy the right atmosphere and sense of togetherness, and neither can you hurry it. *Hygge* is often associated with eating or drinking, but the more it counteracts consumption, the more *hygge* it becomes.

In fact, the more money and prestige is associated with something, the less *hygge* it is! How wonderful is that? Drinking tea is more *hygge* than drinking champers. Playing board games is more *hygge* than computer games. *Hygge* is easier to obtain in Blackpool than Mauritius. Homemade cake is more *hygge* than bought.

Hygge has sounds: crackling bonfires, silent snow, a child drawing or colouring in. Thunder is *hygge* (more so if you're inside counting the seconds between the flash and the rumble). In the olden days we used to unplug the TV aerial if there was a storm, lest the lightning got conducted into the lounge. Sometimes the thrill would be ramped up by a full-blown powercut and we'd sit in candle-lit darkness, me dripping hot wax on my little sister. I'm telling you, life doesn't get more *hygge* than that (admittedly, she might not agree).

Mysa, *Peiskos*, *Hygge*: learn from the happy Scandis. Snuggle into the snuggly moments.

SHINE #10: We Worry 4U™

Here's a thought; *Esquire* magazine's editor, 'AJ' Jacobs, was so busy that he needed a personal assistant. He offloaded all the mundane stuff to start with and, once they'd mastered that, his PA graduated to managing some assignments he didn't fancy. One day, in a flash of enlightenment, AJ realized he was worrying about a big project he was working on, so he decided to outsource the worry.

Let me be clear, he didn't hand over the project, just the fretting. He asked his assistant if she would worry about the project for him, thereby giving him extra time to focus on it in a positive way. She agreed. And every day when he started to ruminate, he'd remind himself that his PA was already on the case and he'd relax.[1]

So here's something no authors on the planet have ever offered their readership. For absolutely no fee whatsoever, we will take on your worry. Yep, the whole burden. Gav will take half and Andy the other. All you need to do is email us at authors@weworry4U.co.uk with a couple of lines about the shit you'd like us to worry about. You can be certain that we'll then worry about it for you, leaving you free to skip along, unburdened and fret-free.

Gav's offering an extra service called '*over-thinking*' (his speciality) in which he'll take your issues and ruminate on them. He'll mull them over and over and over before coming to no final solution, just like you would do yourself. What a wonderful result! You can sleep soundly, safe in the knowledge that Gav isn't. He's in his dressing gown, pacing up and down until 4am.[2]

---

[1] Ferris, T. (2007). The 4-hour Workweek. *Crown Publishers*.
[2] Please note: there is a small charge for this service, which covers Gav's medication.

Our #SHINE10, in all their glory

1. Plot twist!
2. Live a full-ass life.
3. Let it go.
4. Shine-tinted specs.
5. Celebrate stuff that didn't happen.
6. Scratch your itch.
7. Be Chris Tavare.
8. Plenty of the f-word.
9. Get snuggly.
10. We Worry 4U™.

Andy's just this minute decided to add an 11th, yes an 11th-hour one-liner that sums all the others up: *Be the kind of person your dog thinks you are.*

Weird, wonderful and cleverer than they look. Use them wisely.

Chapter 8

CARRY ON THINKING

fishy business awaits you →

So far so good. Most of this book's been an easy-peasy doddle of a read as we skip through sunlit poppy fields of happiness and wellbeing. *Tra-la-la*. All shiney shiney, happy-clappy.

Time to quit your *tra-la-laaing* and ratchet things up. In every personal development book things eventually turn inwards, collapsing in on yourself, getting you to think about your thinking.

Thinking. What is it? What isn't it? How do we end the civil war between our own ears, the 'you versus you' ding dong that inevitably *you* win, beating the crap out of yourself with three falls and a submission?

Note to self: it's very simple to make things difficult and very difficult to make things simple. Andy's spent 12 years of hard academic slog looking at theories. His advice? Never underestimate the power of an insight. Sometimes, an insight is worth all your previous experiences in life put together. In Chapter 8, all we ask is that you keep an open mind. There's an epidemic of depression and mental illness, which is a big pointy finger that something's amiss. If psychology worked, we'd have fewer people in therapy, not more. If meds worked, we'd not need them. So if *more of the same* is out, that leaves room for a Monty Python catchphrase.

Ladies and gents, *and now for something completely different*.

Starting with, *erm*, fish …

Something fishy

Wiki-Fishy-Fact: for clarification, any group of fish that stays together for social reasons is said to be shoaling, and if the shoal is swimming in the same direction together, it is schooling.

Fish get many benefits from shoaling. The community provides defence against predators and it may help a fish find food and a mate. The school can even swim faster than a lone fish.

Mullet (the fish, not the haircut) are among the more spectacular schooling fish. They aggregate together in huge numbers, and 'chains' of mullet schools 100 kilometres long have been seen migrating in the Caspian Sea. There are school rules, very precise arrangements which allow the school to maintain relatively constant cruising speeds.

Schooling is a classic example of 'emergence', where there are properties that are possessed by the school but not by the individual fish. Emergent properties give an evolutionary advantage to members of the school which non-members do not receive.

> 'Just keep swimming. Just keep swimming. Just keep swimming, swimming, swimming. What do we do? We swim, swim.'
>
> *Dory, 'Finding Nemo'*

On to whales. The blue whale is the largest mammal on earth. An adult blue whale is the length of two-and-a-half buses, weighs more than a fully loaded 737 aircraft, has blood vessels large enough for an adult to swim down, a heart the size of a Volkswagen Beetle, and an eight-foot tongue weighing in at 6000 lbs. A little-known fact is that a blue whale is so large that when it decides to turn around, it can take two to three minutes to turn 180 degrees.

But compare the way a blue whale turns around (slowly) to how a school of fish turns around – specifically our mullet described above – which has a greater mass than the whale. A school of mullet can turn almost instantly. The question that crops up is: how do they do this? How do they know when to turn? Indeed, are mullet telepathic?

The answer is simultaneously a little simpler and quite a bit more complex. If you take a careful look at a school of fish, you'll notice that although the fish all appear to be swimming in the same direction, in reality, at any time, there will be a small group swimming in a different direction. Not only different, but opposite, against the flow, against conventional wisdom. And as they swim in another direction, they cause conflict, they cause friction, and they cause discomfort for the rest of the school.

But finally, when a critical mass of truly committed mullet is reached – not a huge number like 50 or 80% of the school, but 10 to 15% who are truly committed to a new direction – the rest of the school suddenly turns and goes with them – almost instantaneously!

Just sayin'. No reason. Yet.

Numbskull

Earlier, Gav explained the science behind his encounter with the *real* Mary Poppins. Well, it seems there's something about Mary because here she is again, but this time an imaginary Mary who crops up in a thought experiment proposed by Frank Jackson.

Imagine, if you will, that Mary is a brilliant scientist who is, for whatever reason, forced to investigate the world from a black and white room via a black and white television monitor. She specializes in the neurophysiology of vision, so she's acquired all the physical information there is to obtain about what goes on when we see ripe tomatoes, or the sky, and uses terms like 'red', 'blue' and so on. Mary discovers, for example, just which wavelength combinations from the sky stimulate the retina, and exactly how this produces, via the central nervous system, the contraction of the vocal cords and expulsion of air from the lungs that results in the uttering of the sentence, 'The sky is blue'.

In other words, 'Mary' is a scientist who knows everything there is to know about the science of colour, but has never experienced colour. The question that Jackson raises is: once she *experiences* colour, does she learn anything new?

It's a similar argument for happiness. We know everything there is to know. We can describe it in some detail. Andy's written a 120k-word thesis about it.

But *experiencing* it is where it's at.

Mary is a brain expert, so she was exposed to pictures such as the one below. You don't need to have any medical expertise to spot the abnormality in this thorax scan. I mean, check it out, it's like body scanning for beginners. The difference between left and right is so stark.[1]

----

[1] *Drew, Vo and Wolfe (2013). 'The Invisible Gorilla Strikes Again.' Psychological Science 24(9),* pp. 1848–1853.

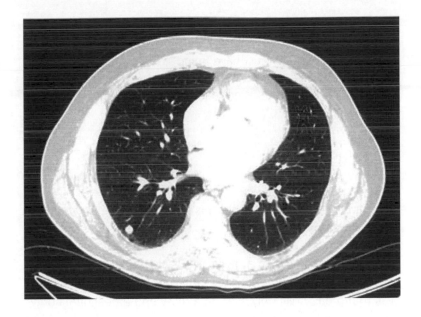

If it took you a bit of time, don't worry. Not an insignificant number of experienced radiologists missed the gorilla in the top-right corner too. We think even Mary might have missed it.

It's yet another pesky example of 'Inattentional Blindness', or what we're snappily calling 'TFtSVaOSEWOiPATSE': *the failure to see visible and otherwise salient events when one is paying attention to something else.*

If we were going to translate it for everyday life, it might be the equally snappy 'MaWCoLaYSoYS' or *'missing a whole chunk of life as you scroll on your smartphone'.*

If we did a similar scan on your head it would show that the brain is biological. It's a wet electrical network, three pounds of jello, an actual thing.

The mind is none of the above. It's spiritual. The brain itself lacks the power to think. Just like your fridge needs electricity to function, so the brain must have 'mind' to make it work.

Still with us? '*Just about*' is good enough.

Onwards …

Carry on inside out

You might need to sit down for this bit. Breaking news: *you are NOT a raspberry*.

As well as being a bit of a relief, this is also a reminder that a raspberry seed will only ever turn into one thing. In the same way that a daisy will only ever be a daisy and a peach will only ever succeed in being a peach, these things are locked into one reality.

But you have a mind, which gives rise to thoughts, which gives you a lot more potential. It can't turn you into a raspberry, but it gives you the power to experience emotions, to think, rationalize and imagine, all skills that elude our illustrious summer fruit.

Consciousness is our ability to be aware of the world. The ability to recognize that we are thinking, to be thinking about what we're thinking, to be thinking about why we're thinking about what we're thinking, and to make choices to stop thinking it.

We can't say for sure, but we're almost certain that raspberries can't do that. We're equally *almost* certain that not only is this level of consciousness not available to any of the soft fruit family, it's a uniquely human thing, so other animals haven't got the ability to think about their thinking.

Consciousness allows us to be aware of our existence. It arises through thought. In fact, it gives you the ability to be aware of thought and to choose between thoughts; in other words, it gives you *freedom* of thought.

Thought is the tool by which we explain the world, communicate our understanding and by which we perceive the world. Thought gives us an ability to create images and form ideas, thus creating our own experience of reality. I think of thought as the paintbrush that you create reality with.

It starts to get interesting when you realize that thought is not reality, but it is through thought that we create our reality. Thought creates emotional states and it's perfectly possible to be held prisoner by your own thoughts. Our minds are inhabited by ANTs: automatic negative thoughts. Our #SHINE10 from Chapter 7 is like ANT-repellent, but you need to know that the ANTs will never go away. The best you can ever do is manage them.

Managed poorly, destructive and negative thoughts will create painful emotions or, worst-case scenario, can kill you. Managed well, helpful, positive thoughts can enrich your life.

The principles above are taken from Syd Banks' so-called 'three principles', which we've slimmed down to two: thought and consciousness. The third one is 'mind' and although Syd would argue the toss, for us, it adds an unnecessary layer of complexity. A word about Syd – a largely unknown Scottish bloke who emigrated to heaven in the 1990s. A shipyard worker on the Clyde, Syd had an epiphany. Well, several really. Various people have tried to espouse Syd's work. Here's our take.

Syd's main point is this: all the solutions to all your problems will be found inside you. The 'trick' is to realize that you already know.

Here it is in one simple sentence, what you might call Syd's elevator pitch: *your thoughts are creating the current state you're in.*

End of.

We're going to set aside any argument about whether that's an original thought, or whether it's Buddhism, mindfulness or whatever. For Syd, who was, by his own admission, an ordinary guy, this was an original thought and, indeed, an extraordinary one.

The queue of happiness

Dr Syd (he wasn't a doc, but we think he should receive a posthumous honorary doctorate from one of the Scottish unis) realized that your feelings never come from what's happening to you. Using his logic, a rainy day can never make you feel bad just as winning the lottery can never make you feel good. Your feelings can only ever come from one source, and that's your thinking.

You are feeling your thinking. You can't have a good feeling with a bad thought, and vice versa.

Syd was a mullet of his time. The reason we like Syd's principles is because they go against the grain of conventional thinking. We tend to think of emotions as real things. We can be the victim of emotions when, of course, we created them in the first place. It's like coshing yourself over the head with a baseball bat and then complaining that your head hurts. Stop coshing yourself and you'll feel a whole lot better.

We're programmed to think *outside in*, or at least to be fooled into thinking that's how it works. If I asked you why you're feeling down, it's because it's Monday, or it's raining, or you've got too much work on. Flip you into happy mode and you'd suggest you're feeling fab because it's the weekend, or your football team's won, or it's sunny.

Let's share one of Andy's big moments, and, like many of his epiphany moments, it happened in and around food.

It was Christmas Eve and my wife was busy preparing for the following day's festivities. She handed me a list and asked if I could just pop to the supermarket. That, of course, was not a problem at all. I mean, how hard could it be?

Except it was mid-morning on Christmas Eve, the busiest shopping hour of the busiest shopping day of the entire year. The superstore was a heaving mass of ruddy-faced stress heads. And, although I only had 10 things on my treasure hunt, they were unusual things (cranberry sauce, marzipan, horseradish, etc.) so it wasn't a shopping list, it was a mystery tour.

Another 45 minutes ticked by and, ankles bashed in by people with trolley rage, I had basketed my items and made my way to pay. So, which queue? This was pre-self-service checkout days so I opted for the '10 items or less' queue and consigned myself to a 20-minute wait. *Shuffle forward. Shuffle forward.*

Five minutes later there was a bit of to-do. The man in front of me had counted the number of items in the lady's basket in front of him, and she had 11 items. Now, on my Richter scale of, 'Do I give a shit?' it was registering a zero. But his needle was oscillating. He challenged her with a rather blunt, 'Can you count?'

The lady looked a little confused. 'Yes,' she said hesitantly, 'of course I can count.'

'So how many items have you got?' he snarled.

There was a moment's silence as she tallied them. 'I'm ever so sorry,' she apologized. 'I see what you mean. I've accidentally gone one over. I hope you don't mind. It's a genuine and honest mistake and, to be honest,' she said, smiling weakly, 'it's Christmas so I'm in a bit of a rush.'

The man stood a little taller, somewhat aggressively I thought. 'We're all in a rush, love,' he growled. 'And it's people like you who ruin Christmases for people like me.' And off he went, effing and blinding and jabbing his finger. Within a few seconds we'd got a full-blown cat-and-dog style argument and everyone in the queue was shrinking into their shoes, avoiding eye contact and wishing they were somewhere else.

The point is that about two minutes into their argument, at the height of the bellowing, when everyone else was shrinking, I had an epiphany. You might say I upped my level of consciousness. I was feeling miserable. And where do feelings come from? None other than my thinking, so I dared to challenge and therefore *change* my thinking. I stood tall and looked around at the supermarket full of food. *How lucky am I to live in the UK? And to have a job and a credit card.* I listened to the argument, nodding in agreement. *They are both right!* I noticed the guy's blood pressure had risen to the point that the vein on his neck was pulsating. *The lady accidentally putting an extra item into her basket might actually kill him!* By the time I got to the cashier I had a serenity and calmness. The lady beeped my 10 items through and I wished her a very merry Christmas, clambering into my car with a massive grin on my face.

I had thoroughly enjoyed that queue and I suspect I was the only one who had. While everyone else had resorted to their default thinking (creating rage, frustration and glumness), I had dared to exercise a choice and this had, quite patently, got me a much better result.

Is the supermarket example a big deal? Yes and no. It's a small incident, but one of a million similar incidents that happen to you and I every day. The way you react to these million incidents colours your life. Now that's big!

Allow us to work through the supermarket situation, showing you the order of events. The *outside-in* version first (remember, this is how most people live their lives).

Technically, the *outside-in* version will operate in this four-step process (remember, this is how most people operate, most of the time):

1. Trigger (long queue).
2. Feeling (unfairness, frustration, anger).
3. Behaviour (impatience, negativity, complaining).
4. Outcome (irritation, stress, ulcer).

The *inside-out* model adds a step:

1. Trigger (long queue).
2. THINKING (how would the best version of me react?).

3. Feeling (upbeat, relaxed, grateful that I am about to buy food for Christmas).
4. Behaviour (calm, positive, smiley).
5. Outcome (enjoying the queue!).

It's a game-changer. But it's also a very slippery concept. The inside-out model means you need to get your head around the fact that all events are neutral. So there are no good or bad queues, until you apply thinking to them. There is no good or bad weather, until you apply thinking. There are no good or bad meetings, until you apply thinking. Workload is neutral, until you apply thinking. The big hurdle is to understand that Mondays and Fridays are totally equal, they're both worth a 7th of your life, and Mondays only become bad when you apply thinking to them. (Yes, we understand how challenging this last one is, because it goes against everything you see around you.)

Its slipperiness comes from the speed of thought. Often, you don't have time to rethink your thinking. It's like sneezing. There are two types of sneeze. There's the long-approaching one which you hope is coming. You want it to come because the situation is right and you know the sensation is going to be just that, *sensational*. Here she comes … what a beauty, a mini orgasm caught safely in your tissue. And there's the other sort, the sudden sneeze that springs a surprise. Not only that but it's the wrong place and the wrong time: a packed train carriage, an interview, a library … no tissue … there's snot shooting across the room before you knew it was coming.

Yes, in an analogy that's never been made before (possibly with good reason), we're suggesting your thinking is even faster than snot globules. The trick with inside-out thinking is to understand it's just a thought. And by 'it' we mean 'everything'. Ever.

Understanding this stuff doesn't make you immune from trauma and unhappiness. It doesn't prevent disappointment. Sometimes bad stuff happens and life doesn't work out. The power comes in realizing you have choices about what to think next. This is what David Taylor calls the 'gap of infinite possibilities'. You have choice, and that gives you power over the situation.

You don't have to wait for your circumstances to change, and that's crucial.

Jaw jaw

Psychologists have developed various 'talking therapies' which (basically) seek to alter you from outside-in to inside-out. Inside-out thinking won't make everything rosy, but it will prevent you taking negative thoughts, even ones that seem viciously real, too seriously for too long. Inside-out's big breakthrough means it's reassuring to know that, whatever your past or present situation, you are only ever one thought away from happiness. This remarkable ability is available to everyone but most are totally unaware of it. It costs nothing and no talent or qualifications are required – just a bit of insight and, from my experience, quite a lot of practice.

At ninja level, inside-out is about less effort. You don't even have to change your thinking, merely to realize that any bad feelings you experience are created by thinking, and another thought will be along in a few seconds. Let that angry one pass and, hey presto, I'm going to jump aboard this positive one instead.

Understanding this doesn't mean you won't get run over by a bus. It means that if you survive the bus incident, you might be better able to deal with the consequences. Ditto all the other more minor stuff that will happen to you: red traffic lights, back-to-back meetings, a rainy day, an irritating mother-in-law, a sullen shop assistant, a flat tyre, a leaky window, too many emails, a five-minute supermarket queue. All these things will continue to happen. Inside-out means you don't have to remain stuck in situations, or trapped in bad thoughts and memories.

But what about trauma? We don't know your history, but there's a strong likelihood that genuinely nasty stuff will have happened at some point. Some individuals seem to have accumulated enough trauma to fill several lifetimes. However, have you noticed that not everyone who experiences extreme trauma suffers from the experience? For a lot of people, a bit of time and space is enough to let the 'ordinary magic' heal them, and they use the bad experience as a springboard for the next chapter of their life.

That's because the way we feel about events in the past depends on the way we think about them in the present. Trauma is a memory carried through time, via thought. It's a horrific event that's hitched a ride on your thoughts.

Inside-out says we cannot change the trauma (the event was real, it was horrible and it really happened) but we can change the story we attach to it. Pondering what happened in the past can trap you there. Everyone can find something awful if we go hunting for it! The more pain you suffer NOW, the less room for happiness and joy NOW. We can only ever change the way we're thinking NOW.

Here's a sentence you might not expect from us – the point is not to eliminate bad thoughts. You can't. But you can realize they're thoughts and let them pass. That way, they can't control you.

We cling to horrible memories and we feel ashamed and embarrassed long after everyone else has forgotten. Remember, everyone else is too busy hanging onto their own shame and embarrassment to be interested in yours!

We class inside-out as an insight rather than a theory. Once you just go with the flow, it can burst open the door of your potential and expose the fact that there's an awesome version of you much closer than you think.

What a cunning hiding place – *inside your head!*

Half-baked?

'Inside-out' is the best self-help 'technique' in the history of the universe, yet almost nobody knows about it and, even in the modern world of social media sharing of everything, it's not gone viral.

The standard criticism of Syd's work is that it's too simple. Or that it's unproven academically. There's a distinct undercurrent in academia and medicine that asserts that depression and misery are more sophisticated emotions than happiness and joy. More worthy perhaps. Psychologists study illness because, somehow, it warrants more analysis than joy. For years the thinking flowed one way: if we study illness, we can find out more about it and use that information to make people better.

We're not saying that's a bad approach, merely that it's half-baked. Look around you. What do you see? How many people are 'off with stress' or suffering from anxiety, panic attacks or depression? Fat people. Unhealthily skinny people. Alcohol-fuelled people. Addicts of all sorts. Low-level misery. There are an awful lot of 'just-getting-bys' who come alive at weekends before sinking back into their torpor from 4pm on Sunday. We trudge to work on a Monday, leaden footed, like Superman with kryptonite down his y-fronts.

Our *thinking* is killing us.

Is misery a more important subject than happiness? If so, tragedy is superior to comedy, dark days warrant more news than sunny ones and people who are happy and content are somehow trivializing life.

We're not saying that people don't suffer. We suffer. But we're not convinced there's any sophistication about long-term suffering. But going to therapy to perpetuate these thoughts seems kind of counter-intuitive. 'Come on in. Have a lie down. Tell me about all the shit in your life …'

Syd Banks suggests therapy is like going in the shower to dry off.

But look around you again, this time with a much keener Six-Million-Dollar-Man-eye. You'll notice something different. Not everyone's doing the same. Remember Andy's sciencey stuff from Chapter 3? There's a small band of people who aren't slouching. They're alive! Even on a Monday morning. Bright-eyed, springy, smiley, optimistic people who come to meetings and light them up with their positivity. They ooze energy and it seems to leak out of them into everyone they meet. They experience the same red traffic lights and back-to-back meetings but, somehow, they shine.

To move from half-baked to fully-baked, surely psychology needs to take note of these people too? Who are the happies? Why are they happy? How do they do it? How do they *maintain* it? Most crucially, what if we studied them, discovered their secrets and applied the remedies to the rest of the population?

Their zest isn't linked to caffeine and sugar. The key ingredient is in their heads – and it's in your head too. There's something inside all of us, but sometimes it lies dormant. There's nothing 'missing' as such, but we've just forgotten about it. Imagine if you didn't require a therapist, priest or plastic surgeon, but instead just allowed your inner wisdom to shine through.

The truth is this: if there's something missing in your life, it's probably you.

Too often our inner wisdom is clouded by routine thoughts. Consciousness means you can begin to catch yourself thinking and realize it to be what it is. This gives rise to choice. This doesn't mean we'll make great choices all the time, but when a destructive thought passes through, you know it's destructive and choose not to hang onto it. It's like surfing. Andy tells me he's a good surfer (yeah, right!) but I guarantee that when he goes surfing he doesn't catch every wave, he tries to pick a good one and go with it. Sometimes he picks a wrong 'un and takes a serious tumble. After coughing up a pint of seawater, he's back on the board to try again. Most waves pass by. Catch a good one and punch the air as you ride it as far as you can. Ditto your thoughts. They're going to keep on coming, waves and waves of them, so choose more carefully and start riding the positive ones.

Just realizing and recognizing the power of thought and that you are the thinker is often enough to change the experience of that moment.

We solve problems not by *more* thinking but by shifting out of our regular pattern of thinking. So, while those around you continue to shoal in an outside-in direction, we encourage you to take a closer look at Syd's work. To shine, you have to dare to be the inside-out mullet. Do it, and pass it on.

You cannot force wisdom, all you can do is wait on it. Eventually, the school will learn and the shoal will turn.

Chapter 9

UNRAVELLING STRING THEORY

Spot the similarity...

'Epic' is *sooooo* overused, don't you think?

Welcome to our Bill and Ted chapter, in which epic doesn't even come close to describing its breadth, depth and unfathomability. We grapple with the ungrappleable by diving into the gene pool and introducing a host of concepts you didn't even know that you didn't know that you didn't know about. Hox genes for a start, then transcription factors, DNA promoters and quantum theory in three easy steps.

But, of course, the last bit of that sentence is a lie. We do our darndest and ask you to hang in there when it starts hurting, because we're building your body of knowledge to the point whereby you can amaze, impress and bore the pants off your nearest and dearest.

Look, there's also some cool stuff about the Kia service plan, Mega Mind and juice, but these are small fry alongside the concept of 'elan vital' and our battle cry of 'go love yourself'.

There's a reason why other authors don't go near this shit, right?

Right!

Speedos off, we're going in deep …

Skinny dipping

If the previous chapter was 'Carry on Thinking', this one might be subtitled 'Carry On Up The Ante'. Academically, it's a toughie. But hey, no pain no gain. In this chapter we grapple with rocket science and then something far more complex, quantum theory.

Let's loosen up with rocket science first. Here you go …

'Remember: some small children are frightened by fireworks. Another great way to frighten them is to tell gory ghost stories.'

#ardaghtips

$$\frac{1}{F(p;\xi)}$$

$$= 1 + \frac{\alpha}{\pi p^2} \int_0^\infty dk \frac{k^2 F(k;\xi)}{k^2 + M^2(k;\xi)} \left\{ a(k,p) \left[-\xi \left(1 - \frac{k^2 + p^2}{2kp} \ln \left| \frac{k+p}{k-p} \right| \right) \right] \right.$$

$$+ b(k,p) \left[2(k^2 + p^2) \left(1 - \frac{k^2 + p^2}{2kp} \ln \left| \frac{k+p}{k-p} \right| \right) \right.$$

$$\left. - \xi \left(k^2 + p^2 - \frac{(k^2 - p^2)^2}{2kp} \ln \left| \frac{k+p}{k-p} \right| \right) \right]$$

$$\left. - c(k,p) \left[2 \left(1 - \frac{k^2 + p^2}{2kp} \ln \left| \frac{k+p}{k-p} \right| \right) - \xi \left(1 - \frac{k^2 - p^2}{2kp} \ln \left| \frac{k+p}{k-p} \right| \right) \right] \right\} \cdot \frac{M(p;\xi)}{F(p;\xi)}$$

$$= \frac{\alpha}{\pi} \int_0^\infty dk \frac{k^2 F(k;\xi)}{k^2 + M^2(k;\xi)} \left\{ a(k,p) M(k;\xi) \left[(2+\xi) \frac{1}{kp} \ln \left| \frac{k+p}{k-p} \right| \right] \right.$$

$$+ b(k,p) M(k;\xi) \left[\frac{2(k^2 + p^2)}{kp} \ln \left| \frac{k+p}{k-p} \right| + 2(\xi - 2) \right]$$

$$\left. + c(k,p) \left[\frac{(2+\xi)k^2 + (2-\xi)p^2}{2kp} \ln \left| \frac{k+p}{k-p} \right| + (\xi - 2) \right] \right\},$$

$$(15)$$

Great. And with that cleared up we can turn to quantum theory.

Our problem? Remember Chapter 5 on goal setting? We wanted to raise it from '*A*' chapter on goal setting to '*THE*' chapter. Here, we're attempting to do the same for quantum physics.

We're about to disappear through a quantum tear in the universe, to a world where genes are not puppet masters pulling the strings of your behaviour, but are puppets at the mercy of your behaviour.

Immediately, you feel a chill in the air – our jaunty tone guillotined by a puppet sentence. It's a tricky few words to get your head around. You might have to read it two or three times before it makes any sense. In fact, even then it probably doesn't compute.

But there's something else – puppets are proper scary.
Puppets and clowns. The domestic violence of Punch and Judy is bad enough, but it's likely you've seen a Chucky film. If you're under 30, it'll be Annabelle! Same result. You feel a chill.

Good.

Pull your duvet up to your eyeballs and we'll carry on. This is our 18 Certificate chapter. Anyone who tells you they understand quantum physics is a liar. Even quantum physicists, the lying bastards.

Definition

'Curglaff (Scottish): The bracing, shocking and/or invigorating feeling of suddenly entering (e.g. diving into) cold water.'

Adjust your goggles, we're about to jump into the gene pool. To appreciate this section you need to abandon cherished notions that you learned long ago and keep an open mind. In fact, we'd prefer you to remove your Speedos. It's much more exciting to skinny dip in the gene pool. After all, that's how you started out.

Let's start easy with a game of 'spot the similarity': chimps, humans, mice and giraffes. The differences are a doddle, most notably neck length, size and good looks. The similarities are a lot harder. Mammals for sure. But what else?

If you dive into the gene pool, the answer is that they're all more or less the same. The difference is not in the genes but in the same set of 30k genes used in a different order and pattern.

Yes, you are basically a mouse, assembled in a different way (that explains your midnight cheese cravings).

WARNING!

This book's about to get tough, so here's an activity that will bolster your fortitude, enabling you to carry on when the content starts hurting. Which it will.

In the following family tree, start at the bottom with your name, then the names of your parents, their parents and their parents. There will be eight names on the top row:

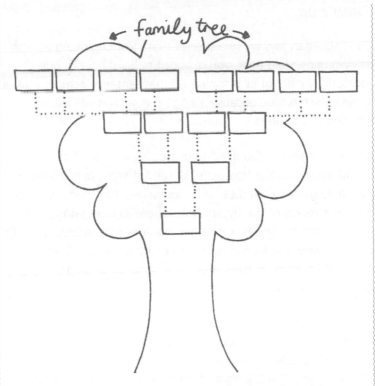

Except, of course, there won't be eight names. Your name? Hopefully that was the easy bit. Your ma and pa, ditto. Your grandparents? Harder. Top row? Rock hard. There's a big fat chance that you don't know the names of your grandparents' mums and dads.

The implications are knee-trembling. *Your great grandkids won't know your name!* They won't know your name but there will be some traits and characteristics passed down.

Here's our promise. Your great grandchildren might not know who you were but, if you read, absorb and embrace the material from this point onwards, they will be grateful.

Saddle up

Dan Eagleman says we're a species that's just beginning to grab its own reins. Hold tight, you're about to learn how to ride ... *yourself*. (Neither of us is convinced that sentence actually makes sense, which is fine, because a lot of this section will leave you scratching your head.)

Concentrate now. You need to grasp this for later. First, let's introduce you to the Hox gene. Wildly different animals have the same genes. Fruit flies have Hox genes that seem to set out the basic recipe of the fly: roughly where its legs, wings and head should be. The Hox is rather like template instructions. If it goes haywire, the fly will have two or three heads. Then those studying mice found the same thing. And guinea pigs, and giraffes ... and us.

That means we all came from the same template; in other words, the Hox came from a long-extinct ancestor that has been preserved forever in all of us. Your Hox makes sure your bits and bobs are all in the right place. It also contains the protein recipes for 'transcription factors', whose job is to switch other genes on.

So, how come some genes get switched on and some off? A transcription factor attaches to a region of DNA called a 'promoter'. It's like the most complex game of chess ever imagined. The promoters can attract blocking or attracting transcriptors, so the gene can be active or dormant. Put more simply, genes can burn brightly, be active but dim, or be stone cold.

Got it? Good. Next level ...

Open book

For most of biological history we've viewed nurture as reversible, hence you can learn new behaviours and habits. We've learned that nature is not. The genes you're born with are the genes you're born with. The genetic book gets slammed shut. That was the end of the story.

> 'Philosophers have flung themselves headlong at the happiness problem for quite some time with little more than bruises to show for it.'
>
> *Dan Gilbert*

We'd like to reopen it, at the halfway point. Is it perhaps half true? The true bit might be that our genetic code is inherited from our parents, so certain aspects such as eye colour, hair colour, body shape and height are fixed. So, your genetic code shapes your body and it gives a *starting point* for your mind.

How your mind *develops* is dependent on which genes get switched on. The 'switching on' part of your development is sensitive to the world in which you live. Thus, the environment switches you on or off.

That sentence needs investigating, so let's do it via geese. There's a critical period, the window when environment acts irreversibly upon the development of behaviour. The best example is goslings. Baby geese latch onto the first living thing they see and that attachment lasts forever. YouTube it for examples of goslings being 'imprinted' on all sorts of weird and wonderful 'mothers'.

We tend to see this as innate behaviour, pre-programmed into the chicks. But the environment has to give the infants something to follow. And they will follow anything, so the gosling is 'open minded' about what mother is, until it is exposed to mother. Thus, the external environment shapes behaviour just as much as internal drive does.

But that's geese, right? What about people? David Barker examined men born between 1911 and 1930, comparing birth weights with death rates from heart disease. Light babies died earlier, leading Barker to conclude that heart disease is less about environmental effects during life and more to do with early development (in this case, body mass during infancy). Thus, the genetic switches are thrown, or not, in the early years. It seems that a malnourished child will have genes arranged such that the person is born 'expecting' to live in a world of lack. Their whole metabolism is geared to being small, hoarding calories and avoiding burning of calories.

Genes are designed to take their cues from nature.

Next level …

The Secret, Brit-style

Rhona Byrne's *The Secret* is the second bestselling self-help book of all time, trailing just behind *The Bible*. *The Secret* is awesome in its overly earnest mish-mash of new-age old-age mysticism. It veers from totally brilliant to unintentionally laugh-out-loud funny, sometimes on the same page.

It's American. Brits tend not to do this kind of stuff. Until now. Here's something never attempted before; we'll call it '*Not So Secret: quantum theory in three easy-peasy steps*'.

Step 1: What's a thought? Where's a thought? How do we locate a thought?

Okay, not so easy-peasy. What we do know is that it's possible to detect weak electrochemical changes that accompany a physical or emotional response. These carry messages through what physicist Nick Herbert calls a 'wet electrical network', which is information 'jumping' across the synaptic gaps in your brain. Thus, a thought causes a physical change in the brain.

Note, this all requires energy. Energy is what you are. Nothing but. When your energy runs out, it's game over.

So let's drill down into energy. Everything is energy. Yes, *everything*. We see physical objects but, at a molecular level, they're fluid. It's weird, but your basic GCSE physics tells you this is true. Everything is made up of atoms and I'm talking so small that your brain can't really comprehend their minuteness.

In order to be able to see the atoms in an average-sized apple, you'd have to enlarge it to the size of the earth. Then its atoms would be the size of cherries.

Hang in there, we're going sub-atomic. When we look *inside* the atom we find it's a nucleus surrounded by empty space. So pretty much full of nothingness. The nucleus is tiny. We'd have to enlarge the sub-atomic particle to the size of a cathedral dome to make the nucleus into the size of a grain of sand.

Let me revise ... enlarging an apple to the size of the earth would mean we would be able to see its atoms. Then we'd have to enlarge its atoms to the size of a cathedral dome to see the sub-atomic particles and, even at that level of magnification, they would be like grains of sand. So 'matter' (that table leg, blade of grass, laptop, bowl of muesli, you, aka 'everything') is basically a bunch of empty space.

Step 2: Often we're presented with an image of atoms as electrons and protons orbiting a nucleus, like planets orbiting the sun. But if we try to measure an electron's speed and position, it becomes impossible. You can only measure one or the other, in what scientists call the 'indeterminate principle'. We can measure how fast but not where (or vice versa). In the quantum world they have to talk about an electron's 'tendency to exist' – and it all starts getting spooky from there on in.

In terms that make sense (but no sense whatsoever), it's like a commentator describing a middle-distance race and being able to tell you where the athlete is or how fast she's running, but not both.

Please note, if your head's not hurting, we're not doing our job properly.

Homing in further, you find a particle is not a 'thing', as such. It's not a speck of something, like a grain of salt or dust. It's energy. Indeed, Werner Heisenberg says, 'The very attempt to conjure up a picture of elementary particles and think of them in visual terms is wholly to misrepresent them'. Koestler is on the same lines with, 'If you want to envision a quantum as a dot then you are trapped. You are modelling it with classical logic. The whole point is that there is no classical representation for it.'

Erm, okay then.

Weirder than weird, the world bestseller *The Secret* is right, everything is in vibration. Yes, even your table leg. The world's solid nature is merely an appearance. Particles or waves, in some strange sense, don't exist when we're not measuring them.

Here's the brain-exploding question – therefore, *does it mean we are creating them simply by looking for them in the first place?*

Step 3: Your brain is a relentless shape-shifter, constantly rewriting its own circuitry Infants' brains are making a crazy number of connections. By the age of two a child has over one hundred trillion synapses – double the number an adult has.

Your brain peaks at age two! It actually has too many connections, so at the point of full bloom it sets about pruning itself. So, at two, anything's possible. Then you start to create 'you'.

As you mature, 50% of your synapses will be pruned back.

Physically, you are constantly changing. New cells are generated, like Dr Who but a whole lot slower. Your red blood cells are replaced every four months and you shed your skin every few weeks. Taste buds can last a matter of hours. Your entire body is replaced every seven years, like a Kia service plan.

Let me say that again. *Every cell in your body is new. Physically, you are 100% renewed every few years.*

What hangs 'you' together is memory. This is the thread that lets you know who you are. It gives you an identity and acts as the core of you.

Earlier, we grappled with consciousness, arguing that it's what enables you to experience your existence. You have a physical you, but there's another you, *experiencing* the physical you. Look in the mirror. Punch yourself in the face. *Ouch!* It hurts, right? There's physical pain, but who's the one *noticing* the pain? Who's the one saying, 'That was a bloody stupid thing to do to yourself. Idiot!'

The flesh-and-blood-you allows the 'you in your mind' to get around town. The 'you' you see in the mirror is merely a means of transport.

Let's add another level of weird to what is already weirdsville. Your brain has no access to the outside world. It's sealed in a dark chamber. Your brain cannot see, hear, touch, taste or feel. Your senses detect stimuli in the outside world and translate them into a language that the brain can understand. So sight, smell, taste, hearing and touch aren't real – they are an electrochemical rendition in a very dark cave.

In the old paradigm, we assume a 'me in here' and a 'world out there'. My 'me' is located in my mind and the world is an external thing. In the quantum field, your consciousness changes (indeed, creates) what you observe.

We've ascertained that everything is made of atoms. Everything is energy. The ghostly shape of sub-atomic energy only takes on a definite shape when you're observing it (i.e. looking at it). So behind you is a shimmering wavy blob of energy, a seething bubbling mass of atoms. It's literally just energy, until you turn your head and make something of it.

This isn't to say that it disappears when we're not looking at it. Only that its form must be brought into focus by us. Nick Herbert says, just like King Midas, everything we touch turns to matter.

So, in a nutshell, quantum physics shows the universe as a potential energy field. Our own minds form part of that field and our consciousness affects it.

Yes, yes, we know. Your head is pounding. Please hang in there, it'll be worth it in a page or two.

This is high-level stuff. Nosebleed level. But we'd like to tempt you higher …

> 'The gradual recognition that what we think may physically influence what we observe has led to a revolution in thought and philosophy, not to mention physics.'
>
> *Fred Alan Wolf*

Cocktails

Scientists keep pushing the boundaries. Apparently, you can remove the nucleus of a cell (enucleation), and it will continue to carry out its function for months so long as it's maintained in a 'culture medium' – a fluid. There's a famous experiment in which a single stem cell was placed into a petri dish, and it self-divided every few hours. After a short while, there were 50k cells, all genetically identical.

The 50k cells were then split into three groups, changing the culture medium (the fluid they live in) for each group. Petri dish #1 formed bone, #2 formed muscle and #3 fat. The cells' formation was not determined by genes, but by the culture medium, aka the environment.

Hence, the environment controls the genetics. Thus, the breaking news is that YOUR GENES AREN'T FIXED. (Well, technically they kind of are, but they're also not. I'll come back to this contradiction in a para or two.)

But how does the environment change the cell? Enter the shiny new science of epigenetics. Do Gav and I understand it? Nope. Does anyone? Probably 'nope' again.

Here's my potted version. Genes have to be activated. They are switched on and off via changes to the cell membrane. Remember, it's not the gene that's crucial, it's the juice it's floating in.

And what are you made of?

Juice!

If you were a product on the supermarket shelf you'd have a long list of ingredients. Bones, purply organy bits, intestines, seven pints of blood, hormones, additives and so on.

Up to the next level of learning, and we can finally get around to the biggest question that literally nobody is asking: *who's in charge of the juice?*

Your mind. It's your Mega Mind that gives the orders. A happy, healthy mind creates a slosh of good thoughts and chemicals that soaks your cells in something nice. This juice switches a set of genes on – the happy ones. The less positive ones remain dormant. They are waiting to be activated by a slew of negative juice (produced by negative thoughts and feelings).

So you have happy, healthy cells. The cells' environment is crucial, but the environment is determined by the mind.

Phew. Got there in the end.

Elan vital

Gav's gone for a lie down. He's chuntering about, 'There's a reason other books don't include this shit Andy ...'

Well that's a shame, because they should. And Gav in foetal position in a darkened room means he will miss the best bit. Human beings are a carrier of what Bergson calls 'elan vital', the creative pulse that lives through all of us. I think of it as the current of life.

Thinking is inevitable. You can't NOT think. Indeed, thinking is a good thing. Or, at least, it can be. But if you spend all your time cursing about the injustices of life, your thinking will be draining you. Rushing, rationalizing, stressing, grumbling and worrying – all the things we're in the habit of doing – are messing with our juices and messing with which genes get switched on and off. The way we think might be blocking our energy. We're like 100-watt bulbs, glowing at 10 watts.

Pixar's 'Inside-Out' isn't a million miles away from the truth. In your head, thoughts are wandering around on the look-out for like-minded pals who they can team up with. So, for example, if you're feeling a bit low, the chances are that 'low' will bump into 'moody' and then join with 'depressed', 'anxious' and lethargic'. Before you know it, they've ganged up and ridden 'happiness' and 'positivity' out of your mind completely.

Your mind has a pipeline of thoughts that keep coming in a steady stream. It can be like a Victorian sewage pipeline, clogged with turds. Or it can be a fresh, clean pipeline, flowing with a gushing stream of positivity and appreciation.

How it hangs

So, here goes, the entire reason for writing this book, to lure you this far and blow your mind with something epigenetic. Remember, we've come clean and admitted that we don't quite understand epigenetics – what with it being a brand-new strand of science, hideously complex and unfathomable to everyone except a few white-coated academics with extra-large foreheads. The fact we don't quite understand it means we're working astonishingly hard to bring you a chapter that is almost understandable.

Keeping the most complex science as simple as possible, your genes are your biological script that is copied in every cell. But the genes are asleep, until their script is read. Your genes are cultivated, or wakened, by your thinking.

A happy, healthy mind produces happy, healthy cells. And vice versa. It boils down to this: having healthy and positive thoughts is more than a nice feeling. These thoughts will trigger certain genes into action, thus re-wiring your brain and changing your life for the better. So, it's true that your genes are fixed. But epigenetics explains that the *sequencing* of your genes (which ones are switched on and off) is down to your thinking.

Therefore, positive emotions (remember, these can only ever come from one place, your thinking) are not just 'nice to have' or something you should reserve for Friday evening. Training yourself to be more positive will create more happy/positive thoughts, which create uplifting emotions, which alter which genes are switched on and off.

Why are we telling you this?

Because it links with our earlier point that you might be trapped inside the contemporary hamster wheel, grumbling that 'it's not fair', and you'd be bang on correct. *It's not!* Remember our point from earlier? Nobody ever said it was. Often people are suffering and creating stress for themselves by thinking, *'Why is this happening to me?'* Bad traffic happens to everyone. So does being dumped. Ditto having a massive row with your partner, camping in the rain and queuing at the checkout.

Suffering, therefore, is not because life is difficult but because people were expecting life to be easy. It isn't. Get over it! Remember the section on plot twists? That's part of the fun!

But the much bigger point is that being stuck in the hamster grumble wheel will be re-wiring your brain towards negativity. And my goodness, it's easy to get stuck there!

> 'Expecting the world to treat you fairly because you are good is like expecting the bull not to charge because you are a vegetarian.'
>
> *Dennis Wholey*

Go love yourself

In true Columbo style, there's just one more thing. Most people go their entire 4000 weeks under-estimating just how important relationships are. There's a particular type of relationship, a 'secure attachment', which is especially crucial. If you're lucky enough to have developed decent bonds with your parents, psychologists would say that you've developed secure attachments and you'll feel relatively safe and stable. This is more important than it sounds because your brain circuitry is designed to keep you safe. Once this most basic need is sorted, you can then start to take a few risks and explore your potential. If you haven't developed secure attachments, your brain is continuously scanning for danger. You're more jumpy, fearful, doubtful and less inclined to take risks.

The world is pretty scary for most people. If you've not developed secure attachments, it can be a juddering ride through the ghost train of life.

But what the textbooks don't ever tell you is that the most important secure attachment you'll ever create is with yourself. Bonding with yourself is the first step. Easy to say, harder to do. Learning to love yourself, for some, is a never-ending journey. Not 'love yourself' in a sense of thinking you're better than anyone else, but 'love yourself' as in making peace with yourself and being comfortable in your own skin.

Once more, one of the tricks is to quit the social comparison race. Let's put it across in a way that you won't have heard before. Comparing yourself to others is just plain ungrateful. You have a body. It was given to you. You didn't ask for it. It's a gift. So to all of a sudden look at someone else's body and wish you had what they've got, is rude to your own body.

So, you do have to fall in love. *With yourself. The self in your head.*

A lightbulb is useless until it's plugged in. It needs connecting to a force. In the same vein, you need connecting to an energy force and, in case you haven't twigged, that energy force is you.

Here's the reason we wrote this book, to lure you to these two sentences. *You shine brightest when you're being your best self. Indeed, the quality of the relationship with yourself determines the quality of your relationship with everyone else.*

Thank you.

Chapter 10
A NEW BEGINNING

All good things come to an end. Bad ones do too. As does life. As will you.

Hence, we start our final chapter with death. And we end it with death. And then there's the Titanic, so more death! Thank goodness for Johnny and David Bowie, sandwiched in between.

Thank you for reading this far. You're in for a treat ...

Is this the best you can do?

It's hard to believe that this is Gav's first book. It certainly won't be his last. I've learned that he's a proper canny Scotsman, a wily old trickster of cunning and productivity. Reminder: me, the Englishman, has 30 published books to my name. Three. Zero.

> 'All we have to decide is what to do with the time given to us.'
> *Gandalf*

The Scotsman? None. Zilch. Null points.

So I took charge and sent him my half of this manuscript and he emailed back with a one-liner: 'Copey, is this your best work?'

And I'm like, *cheeky sod.* But, wanting to keep a feeling of entente cordiale I pinged a one-liner back: 'No Gav, on reflection, I can probably do better.'

Cue two more feverish weeks of me being hunched over a keyboard. I click 'send' again.

This time there's a lot of waiting. Two weeks of it in fact. I damned this creative collaboration, and then one day I logged on and there's an email from Gav. 'I ask you again Copey, is this really the best you can do?'

Crikey! I'm getting a bit sweaty. Gav's standards are ridiculous. *Is it really the best I can do? Jeez, which bit doesn't he like?* On reflection, there are a couple of bits I can tweak so I email Gav with 'No boss, I can improve a bit more.'

Six days later a new, improved document zings its way from Derby to Edinburgh. This time I've attached it with a short message. 'Gav, this is awesome. It's the very best I'm capable of.'

I wait, eyes fixed on the screen and PING, Gav replies in less than 10 seconds: 'In that case Copey, this time I shall read it.'

Ladies and gentlemen, it's been a pleasure to have been 50% of your writing team, but It's time for me to step aside. Our epic finale is crammed with Gavisms. Brace yourself for full-octane, high-energy, self-help comedy that just happens to be deadly serious.

Sit back and relax while the flying Scotsman reaches full steam …

My father's last words …

I got the phone call at 6am. It was my mum and it was grave. 'You need to come now.' I had known for some time this call was coming and yet I still wasn't prepared. Are we ever really prepared for *that* call?

The doctor wasn't expecting my dad to last much longer, so I needed to get to the hospital. And fast. I was due to be giving a speech that morning at a school in the Scottish Borders. I had to phone a colleague and tell him what was happening; he told me to get off the phone and go, he'd take care of things at work. I hung up the phone and as I turned around my wife Ali handed me a bag with a few items of clothing and some toiletries. 'Just go.' I hugged her and ran out the door.

My dad had been rushed to a hospital two hours from where I live. My biggest fear was that I wouldn't make it in time to say goodbye. A few speed limits broken, I made it to the hospital, parked up and ran past the phalanx of pyjama-clad smokers, some with drips attached to their arms. I continued to sprint along hospital corridors, following the blue line, up three flights of stairs towards Ward 8. Double doors ahead, I stopped and sucked in a few lungfuls of air. I knew that on the other side of those doors was my absolute hero, my best friend, my dad. And I was about to see him for the last time.

My brother had got there before me. He and my mum sat in silence. They left the room and gave me time to sit and speak with the old man. Pumped full of morphine and with very shallow breathing, he was completely unresponsive. I didn't care. I said all the things I wanted to say and kissed him on the forehead.

Hours passed. Dad remained unconscious.

Several hours later, having been sat around him sharing memories and telling stories from years gone past, my dad's eyes shot open. He lifted his head off the pillow, looked at mum, looked at my brother, turned to me and said …

'What the fuck's going on?'

He closed his eyes and slipped away.

They were his very last words. 'What the fuck's going on?'

He was the coolest dad in the world, right to the very end. I don't want to overanalyse his immortal last sentence, but could it be that my old man, who I assumed knew everything about everything, knew nothing about anything?

It's generally accepted that life is not a rehearsal. This may explain why a lot of people seem to be making a total hash of it. They're just making it up as they go along. What if we're all just bumbling along in the dark, like Theseus, but without any string to follow?

So what the fuck is going on? We think the short answer to that is *nobody actually knows.*

Go back to the year 1244 and you could predict, with some certainty, what the world would be like in, say, 1280. Anyone who makes that sort of prediction nowadays is off their rocker.

In a world of uncertainty, just one thing is certain. Super-wellness, or shining, is never going to go out of fashion. Whatever the future holds, being the very best version of yourself is the key. It always has been and it always will be. It's the key to staying sane. It's the key to enjoying the hurly burly of life. And it's the key to unlocking the shine in others.

Get gritty

We've all got that friend. You know, the one who's a legend. They're crazy but they're awesome. Let me tell you about my best friend. We'll call him Jonny, because that's his name.

> 'I try to be available for life to happen to me.'
> *Bill Murray*

It was my first year at university and I hadn't even known Jonny six weeks. We were in a particularly boring early-morning lecture and the lights went off as the lecturer hit the play button on a short video for us all to watch.

Jonny was sat to my right. 'I'm going to take off all my clothes,' he said.

I laughed at the ridiculousness of this statement. Crazy, right?

Two minutes later I turned to my right and there's Jonny with zero clothes on. Sitting stark bollock naked in a lecture theatre surrounded by 200 other students.

About four minutes later the video ended and the lights came back on. Jonny, fully clothed once again, turned, gave me a nudge and simply said, 'See, told you I was going to take off all my clothes'.

Why did Jonny do this? It's crazy, right? Crazy, or genius?

The craziest part for me was actually that I didn't see, hear or feel him taking his clothes off! It was like they just fell off and then somehow fell back on again.

How boring would life be if we didn't have that outrageous experience or bold companion or ridiculous story?

As Laura Argintar writes, 'Crazy friends make the best friends. They're the ones who stand out, whose shared memories are always two parts fun and one part completely horrifying.'

I could fill an entire book with 'Jonny escapades', though most I wouldn't be allowed to tell you. But, strangely enough, this chapter's not about persuading you to get your kit off during your next cinema trip or convincing you to be two parts fun and one part horrifying, it's about David Bowie. The actual, real David Bowie …

Before we get to Bowie, a teacher of mine once posed the following question: if there are ten birds sitting on a washing line and five decide to fly away, how many are left?

The whole class screamed, 'Five! Durr!'

Sir smiled and gave us the answer. 'Ten,' he purred. 'They're all still on the washing line.'

We all looked at each other with a puzzled expression.

He continued, 'They only decided to fly away, they didn't actually fly.'

The lesson here, of course, was lost on most of us eight-year olds at the time but later on in life it was very clear. How many times in life do we *decide* we're going to do something and then we don't. We put it off, we find an excuse not to do it.

Learn a musical instrument, change job, stop smoking, lose weight, get fit, ask that person out, get divorced, get hitched, get more sleep, go on *that* holiday, start your own biz, write a book, the list goes on.

But you don't do it. Why? Because you'll get round to it later? Or because you can't? Fear of failure perhaps? Or what others will say? They might even laugh. It's too much like hard work. Things will work out the way they are. You're scared. It's another list that tends to go on a bit.

If you take a closer look, you'll find it's nothing more than a list of excuses. Excuses are what stop you in your tracks. SHINE has been about changing your mindset away from, 'What's the worst that could happen?' to 'What's the best?'

There are two types of people though. Those who then act upon it and those who don't, they just sit around hoping one day it will happen all by itself. In a previous book, Andy described life as a massive DIY project. Just as your IKEA Billy bookcase won't assemble itself and your spare room won't give itself a lick of paint, your life won't move forward without some effort. But the birds on a wire conundrum hints that 'deciding' and 'doing' are not the same thing.

We love Angela Duckworth's grit formula, in which effort counts twice.

First up, *talent × effort = skill.*

When you consider individuals in identical circumstances, what each achieves depends on just two things: talent and effort. Talent relates to how fast we can improve in skill. Applying it to a subject, say maths, a little bit of talent is useful, but talent without effort means you'll never get skilful.

But also, *skill × effort = achievement.*

Once you've got skilful, it's effort that makes the breakthrough to achievement.

Oscar-nominated actor Will Smith articulates it well by admitting that he never really considered himself as talented: 'Where I excel is ridiculous, sickening work ethic.' He goes on, 'I will not be outworked. You might have more talent than me, be smarter than me, you might be sexier than me. You might be all of those things. You got me in nine categories. But if we get on the treadmill together, there's two things. You're getting off first, or I'm gonna die. It's really that simple.'

Deciding to do something is common. Indeed, enthusiasm is common. Endurance is rare, because it takes effort to keep going.

It's a whole lot easier to stop. *And that's the problem.*

Rebel rebel

We've been thinking about the birds on a wire conundrum. We think Sir might have been wrong. If there are 10 birds sitting on a washing line and five decide to fly away, how many are left?

What if the answer is nine? There are nine birds left sitting on the washing line.

Why nine?

Because there's always one. Jonny is one. Mary Poppins is one. David Bowie was one. Not only is there always one but there has to be one. Or else who do we follow? Who lights the way?

We all need a David Bowie. Think about it, someone actually decided to be David Bowie. The guy who decided to be David Bowie was David Robert Jones. He didn't put it off, or panic about what his mates might say, he just became the *actual* David Bowie.

Caitlin Moran describes it thus: 'In 1968, Bowie was a gay, ginger, bonk-eyed, snaggle-toothed freak walking around South London in a dress, being shouted at by thugs. Four years later, he was still exactly that – but everyone else wanted to be like him, too.'

If David Bowie can make being David Bowie cool, we're sure you can make you cool.

Plus, unlike David Bowie, you get to listen to David Bowie for inspiration.

So you're one up on him, really.

Yes, *you're already ahead of David Bowie.*

And so to our Epic ending. And it really is Epic, with a capital 'E'.

'We don't want to ruin the ending for you but everything is going to be magic.'

Gav

The previous 46 700 words have been about rescuing you from a suffocating state of the mundane. We've done what authors do and used the subtleties of language to challenge your thinking. Are you experiencing happy days or muddling through in a *happy daze*? Are you befuddled by a career in which you feel you're embroiled in *busy-ness* instead of business? You could be in *the* right state or *a* right state, the difference is palpable. And there's much less nuance between being well off and experiencing wellbeing.

Just so there's no confusion, to truly SHINE we're nudging you towards happy days, business, *the* right state and wellbeing.

But with 300 words left, let's stop the clever words and fancy author trickery. Let's do some

'The pen is mightier than the sword and considerably easier to write with.'

Marty Feldman

hit-you-between-the-eyes stuff. We started this chapter with death, so let's finish it that way, but, as has been our way since Chapter 1, with some quirkiness.

Congratulations. You're going to die.

You're so lucky to get to die. Because that means you've had the chance to live. Most people are never going to die because they are never going to be born. The potential number of people who could have been here in my place is so huge you'd have to count to infinity, *twice!* And yet here we are, seven billion of us, jostling for position. I don't know about you but I don't feel like some sort of person to be marked out as deserving of life. I have a palpable sense of ordinariness, yet I'm part of the privileged few who've won the lottery of birth against all the odds.

You're the chosen one. You're here. Now. *Alive!* Don't you owe it to all the ones who would have loved to have been born, but never made it, to at least sing and dance a little? And maybe at least try and make a bit of a dent in the universe.

> 'It's everybody's duty to give the world a reason to dance.'
>
> *Kid President*

Putting effort into living life to the fullest, rather than just getting by, means you will shift to what Andy calls 'healthy functioning' – and it's contagious. It attracts and engages others. Some people are naturals in their positive outlook, others might require a bit of extra help, but we're all capable of it.

Our final truth is that everyone has the ability to shine, yet not everyone does. Using the analogy from a few paragraphs ago, there are a lot of birds, sitting on a lot of wires. *Waiting!*

And waiting …

And, you know … waiting.

Your job is simple. It's not to decide, it's to do. Quit waiting. This is your time. Take the weight off your shoulders. Your job is not to inspire anyone else, it's simply to *be inspired*.

SHINING is your purpose!

Think about it. There were passengers on the Titanic who turned down the opportunity of the sweet trolley. The best way of preparing for death is to have a cracking life, so let's finish with an interesting question: *where were you before you were born?*

Because after your energy runs out, there's a fair-to-middling chance that you're going to go back there. It's not a bad place, or a good place, just your energy shape-shifting.

Gav's dad doesn't know what the fuck's going on. Neither do we.

But while you've got some time and energy, it seems sensible to shine.

Full. Fucking. Beam.

About the authors

Gav's bio – written by Andy

Part child, part David Bowie, Gavin lives in Edinburgh, Scotland with his wife and two young children. He is one of the most talented and sought-after keynote speakers on the entire planet. I promise you; I've seen plenty, and Gav's yer man.

He's somehow mastered the art of transporting audiences back to when they were five years old, a magical time filled with wonder and zero fear. He also happens to be an award-winning entrepreneur, award-winning comedian and best-selling children's author. His inspiration comes from where he began his career … primary school teaching.

Email: gavin@gavinoattes.com
Twitter: @gavinoattes
Web: www.gavinoattes.com

Andy's bio – written by Gav

Top bloke. Older and wiser than me (but not quite as funny).

Andy's somehow managed to pen a whole range of books, from the best-selling *Spy Dog* series (he describes himself as world famous if you're 7¾) through to teenage titles and a raft of personal development titles for grown-ups. Oh, and he's sneaked in a PhD in Happiness as well as doing his day job of wowing audiences with his keynote and workshop delivery. His delivery of 'The Art of Being Brilliant' is something to behold.

The man's a machine!

He lives in middle England with his lovely wife and two grown-up kiddywinks.

Email: andy@artofbrilliance.co.uk
Twitter: @beingbrilliant
Web: www.artofbrilliance.co.uk

Index

2%ers 63–5, 67–8
25th, invoking your 36–7
4000-week lifespan 22–3

abnormal, being 8
academics 28
action, taking 111
Adams, Douglas 14
Aiken, Mary 28, 32
Animal Farm (Orwell) 13–14
ant-eaters 18–19
anxiety 5, 11–12, 48, 62–3,
    179–80
apathy 144
Ardagh, Philip 128, 186
Argintar, Laura 210
Asda, not an option for the
    Hazda 131
assholes
    letting other people be 146
    not being one yourself 69
atoms 193–4, 196
automatic negative thoughts
    (ANTs) 171

'Back to the Future' 104
bad stuff that hasn't
    happened 149–50
Baggins, Bilbo 19, 21

Banks, Syd 171–2, 179, 180, 182
Barker, David 192
Batman 45, 93
The Beatles 145
Beer, Ragnar 10
blank page, for drawing your
    'wild things' 103
Blue Monday 46–9
boredom 13
'botheredness' 106–8, 111,
    113, 115, 116, 144
Bowie, David 211, 213–14
brain 123–7, 147–8, 168–70,
    193, 195–6, 200–2
Brashares, Ann 4
broccoli 83
Brown, Les 68
Brown, Stuart 86–7
Browning, Guy 152
Buddha 15–16, 22
busyness 19–21, 214
butter, scraped over too much
    bread 19, 21
buttocks, living a one-buttock
    life 116
Byrne, Rhona 192

Cameron, Kim 63–4, 65–6
Carr, Alan 143

Carr, Nick 35
change 126–7, 135
children 29–32, 33, 77–8,
    79–85, 86
choice 71–2, 151, 177, 181
conformity 61
consciousness 71–2, 170–1,
    181, 195–7
cortisol 11–12
creativity 78, 86, 87–8, 91–2,
    120, 130
cricket 156–7
criticism 157–8
Csikszentmihalyi, Mihalyi 88
cyber effect 32

Dahl, Roald 54
death 120, 205, 207–8, 215
  best way of preparing
    for 216
  funerals 23–4, 69, 90
  hastened by lack of
    sleep 134
  heart disease 192
  as a long vacation 48
déjà vu 146
Delaney, Gary 20
Depersonalization Disorder
    (DPD) 121–2
depression 12, 46–7, 62–3,
    121, 123, 179–80, 199
diet 119, 126, 131–3

DiMaggio, Joe 84
dogs, being the kind of person
    your dog thinks you
    are 162
Dostoyevsky, F. 143
dreams 100, 104, 109
Duckworth, Angela 212
'Dumbo' 81

'e-personality' 27, 32
Eagleman, Dan 190
effort, making an 123, 126, 212
Einstein, Albert 112
elan vital 199
emotions 62–5, 121, 172–3
  emotional energy 65–6, 68
  play 91
  positive 200
  resilience 140
empathy 32, 33–4, 121
energy 6, 60, 130, 144
  2%ers 63–4
  blocking 199
  depletion of 68
  engagement 67
  four types of 65–6
  quantum theory 193, 196–7
  sharing stuff 82
  super-wellness 120
engagement 63, 64–5, 67
environmental influences
    191–2, 197–8

epigenetics 200
eustress 39–40
excitement 4–5, 7, 64, 66, 82, 84
excuses 211–12
exercise 127, 132
    see also running

failure 5, 158–9
family tree activity 188–9
fatigue 79
fear 5, 48
Feldman, Marty 214
'Finding Nemo' 166
fish 166–7
forgiveness 145, 146
fuel, filling up with 40–2
lull-ass life, living a 143–4
funerals 23–4, 69, 90

Gandalf 206
'gap of infinite possibilities' 177
geese 191–2
genes 188–92, 197–8, 200
Gilbert, Dan 191
giving up 125
goals 88, 104–11, 112–13
Godin, Seth 62
grit 141, 212
'growing up' 81

habits 17–18, 125, 126, 127
habituation 98

Hannibal, from the 'A-Team' 8
happiness 11, 23, 60, 71, 199
    2%ers 63, 64
    experiencing 168
    healing yourself with 45
    inside-out thinking 177
    philosophers 191
    relationships as the
        cornerstone of 33
    sleep linked to 134
    world league tables 159
Hazda tribe 131–3
health 119–23, 126, 131–3
'healthy functioning' 215
Hein, Piet 158
Herbert, Nick 193, 196
The Hitchhiker's Guide to the
        Galaxy (Adams) 14
Hox gene 190
Huge Unbelievably Great Goals
        (HUGGs) 108–11, 112–13
'human doings' 21
hunter-gatherers 79, 131
hygge 160
Hyner, David 108–9

identity 18
ikigai 153–5
imagination 91–2, 120
Inattentional Blindness 169
'inner Jeeves' 126–7, 128–9, 130
inner wisdom 181

innovation 91–2
'Inside Out' 199
inside-out thinking 23, 175–9, 182
Instagram 30
internet 9, 10, 30–1, 32, 34, 35–6
  see also social media
invoking your 25th 36–7
Irritable Bastard Syndrome 134, 152

Jackson, Frank 168
Jacobs, AJ 161
'Jeeves, inner' 126–7, 128–9, 130
jerk, not being a 62

Kardaras, Nicholas 35
Kid President 215
Kipling, Rudyard 14
Kor, Eva 146

Layard, Richard 33
layers 16, 60
letting go 145–6
lifespan of 4000 weeks 22–3
London Marathon 129–30
loving yourself 202

magic
  'ordinary' 141, 178
  'wee piece of' 81–2

Manson, Mark 120
materialism 23
mealtimes 34, 132
memory 148, 195
Mercury, Freddie 13
Minchin, Tim 11
mind 198, 200
mobile phones 28–9, 30–1, 34
Mondays 6, 46–9, 60, 173, 176
mood hoovers 68, 69
Moran, Caitlin 213
Morrison, Jim 61
motivation 113–14
Murray, Bill 42, 209
Murray, W.H. 109
music 53, 115–16

narcissism, epidemic of 32
negativity 69, 106–7, 147–8, 157, 201
'neo-Stoicism' 149
neuroplasticity 124–6
news 27, 38–9
ninja turtles 88
'normal', being 6–7, 93

obesity 79, 123, 131–2
Occelli, Cynthia 84
offense, taking 38–9
one-buttock life, living a 116
'online disinhibition effect' 32

opportunity cost 35–6
Optimus Prime 17
'ordinary magic' 141, 178
'outrage porn' 38–9
outside-in thinking 23, 173,
    175, 182
over-engineering 105

pain 107, 140–1, 143, 178, 196
passion 82, 115–16, 144, 154,
    155
perseverance 141
physical energy 65–6, 68
'plastic paradox' 125–6
play 85–92
plot twists 142–3, 201
political correctness 122–3
Poppins, Mary 57–9, 64, 74,
    167–8, 213
positivity 63–4, 71–2, 180,
    199, 200
pronoia 61, 73
psychological energy 65–6, 68
purpose 144, 152

quantum theory 187, 192–7
quests 69, 70

relational energy 65–6
relationships 33, 66, 67, 86,
    201–2
resilience 67, 91, 120, 140

rice krispies, mushy 5
Roberts, Hywel 108
rumination 92, 161
running 127–30
RuPaul 60

sacrifice 107
sadness 12, 66, 140
'sameyness' 98–9
satisfaction 63, 64, 67
Scandinavian countries 159–60
The Secret (Byrne) 192, 194
secure attachment 201–2
self-remembering 60–1
Sendak, Maurice 99–102, 104
sense of smell, related to size
    of willy 10
Seto, Michael 31
sex 10
sharing stuff 82
'Shawshank Redemption' 8
shine-tinted specs 146–8
shit
    accumulating a lot of 16
    cleaning it off your
        spectacles 73
    feeling 140
    happiness through
        pooing 119
    magicking shit out of
        nothing 37
    in the news 38

shit (*cont.*)
  outsourcing your worry 161
  same old or crazy new 3
  shit situations 68–9
  subtractive psychology 17
  unicorns, fun, magic,
    rainbows and 7
  vlogging about a shit
    life 122
Simpson, Homer 92
Sinek, Simon 31
sisu (perseverance) 141
skills and talents 154–5, 212
slacktivism 33
sleep 133–5, 136
'sleight of word' 28
Smith, Linda 141
Smith, Will 212–13
snowflake generation 31
snuggles 159–60
social media 9, 27, 35–6, 157
'South Park' 27
Spy Dog 109
stories 69, 142–3, 145–6
strengths 112–13, 116
stress 5, 11–12, 27, 155,
    179–80, 201
  fake 40–2, 44, 45–6
  good 39–40
  negativity bias 147
  real 143
  sleep as antidote to 134

subtractive psychology 16–17
success 23
suffering 143, 178, 180, 201
Sunday Blues 48
super-wellness 121, 131, 209
superpowers 92–3, 106, 111

Tavare, Chris 156–7
Taylor, David 177
teachers 54–9
Thailand 15–16
thinking 165, 170–82, 199,
    200
Thurman, Howard W. 150
Tig 88–91
time
  4000-week lifespan 22–3
  Gandalf's wisdom 206
  invoking your 25th 36–7
  mapping 18
  not enough time in the
    day 133
toilet-roll holders 42–4
trauma 178
The Troggs 99
Twitter 20, 32

ultracrepidarianism 134

Vardy, Jamie 108
vlogging 121–2
vujà dé 146–7

watches, over-engineered 105
weaknesses 112, 113
'wee piece of magic' 81–2
wellness 120
  see also super-wellness
whales 166–7
Where the Wild Things Are
    (Sendak) 99–100
Wholey, Dennis 201
'wild things' 99–104, 110–11,
    112–13, 115, 116
willies, size of 10
Wolf, Fred Alan 197

Wonka, Willy 19
work 6, 20, 44–5, 48
  emotions 62–5
  play compared with 87
  quitting your job
    150–2
  working hours 10–11
worry 5, 161

youthfulness 79

Zander, Ben 115–16
Zappa, Frank 151